The Sky's the Limit

Applying
Radical
Architecture

gestalten

//UNStudio
MUMUTH House for
Music and Music Theater

Form Finding and Place Making:
The Evolving Role of Sculptural Architecture in the Built Environment

by Sofia Borges

Cities need icons. Icons instill within us a sense of place and collective identity, helping personalize and humanize our built landscape. From the great temples of Southeast Asia to the Mayan pyramids of Central America, iconic structures remains a ubiquitous and recurring architectural manifestation, transcending continents, cultures, and eras.

As the modern city formed and densified, new and impressive structures were built to attract people and business. Beginning with early examples, including the Eiffel Tower and the Crystal Palace, and continuing with the Sears Tower and the St. Louis Arch, cutting-edge acts of design ingenuity and structural prowess have helped put many a city on the map. While the act of branding cities with structural and visual marvels is not a new phenomenon in itself, the appropriation of this marketing technique by private enterprise remains a relatively current development in the life of the icon.

Over the last 30 years, large corporations and public institutions began to realize and exploit the economic and political potential for expanding their branding through architecture. Expedited in 1997 by the remarkable success of Frank Gehry's Bilbao museum and its corresponding "Bilbao effect" that rocketed an unknown Spanish port town into the global spotlight, the creation of city identities through architecture became not only a reflection of the cultural value of a given place, but also a strategic marketing tool. Suddenly, the development of a meaningful cultural landmark became synonymous with securing a big-named architect (starchitect) to design a life-size urban metaphor.

In associating a building with anything from a pair of pants to a massive bird's nest, the distinction between icon and object began to blur. Charles Jenks, one of the founding fathers of the postmodernist movement expands on the growing importance of architectural symbolism as he argues:

"People invariably see one building in terms of another, or in terms of a similar object; in short as a metaphor. The more unfamiliar a modern building is, the more they will compare it metaphorically to what they know." [1]

With this rise of the metaphor, the icon transformed into not only an expression of power, but also into a cunning branding technique that relies on stardom on the one hand and sculptural gestures on the other. By giving the city something identifiable and then linking it back to a brand or corporation, the distinction between business model and city model are drawn ever closer together. The embrace of the icon as a branding commodity quickly cluttered the global skyline with a preponderance of unique, glittering, and entirely self-referential monuments. Soon, the anomaly became altogether anonymous. This overexposure of seemingly one-of-a-kind expressions of steel and glass led to a glut in the market, casting a dull haze over the architectural field.

Corresponding with the economic collapse of 2008, the fashionable movement of expensive, highly legible power towers came to an abrupt halt. With the skyline saturated, countless projects were left partially completed and even more were cancelled before execution. From this professional standstill, and the dire necessity that came with it, arose an opportunity to remake the image of both the icon and the architectural field simultaneously.

In spite of significant financial setbacks, like a great phoenix, the icon has emerged from the ashes, proving more resilient and relevant than ever before. Although the economic intent of building an icon hasn't changed greatly, the way one operates to achieve that goal and the way one addresses and engages the public in the process has shifted significantly. Since the beginning of the economic crisis three and a half years ago, the nature of what an icon can be and what it should look like has been called into question. Although only a few fortunate cities can still afford a recognizable architectural brand like Frank Gehry, smaller and more obscure regions are adopting similar eye-catching techniques at a fraction of the price and pomp. No longer does the icon need to take the form of just another undulating sculpture in the sky; it can instead encompass much broader and experiential alternatives.

While iconic architecture has remained a contentious issue for a number of decades, the rebirth of the icon offers exciting new opportunities for sculptural architecture. The contemporary manifestation of this building typology differs dramatically from the great skyscraper race of the twentieth century in developing industrial cities, as defined by the "duck" (building as sign) and "decorated shed" (building with sign) models made famous by Robert Venturi and the postmodernist movement of the late 1970s and 80s.[2] The key difference between these highly figural and diagrammatic examples of the past and what is happening now lies in the overall approach to the treatment of these iconic buildings.

Up until just a few years ago, the building as sculpture seldom permeated the interior. By mastering the art of the sculpture, architects had mistakenly stripped their buildings of any sculptural qualities. Although it might appear like the most exciting duck or decorated shed from the outside, from within, these projects served as little more than utilitarian shells with generic detailing and floor plates. This trend of symbolic façade-making resulted in a style of architecture where the structure's significance related exclusively to the image of itself, with little concern placed on the surrounding context and city fabric.

Given these evolving design parameters and a growing sense of social accountability, a crazy form is no longer enough. With this superficial approach to architecture now almost completely out of style thanks to the high-profile failure of utopian models like Dubai, architects are shifting their focus toward developing spatial experiences that enhance and correspond with their sculptural forms. A newfound importance is being placed on exciting interiors and buildings that treat the inside and outside as a cohesive and unified gesture integrated within the landscape. These enticing new forms explore what it means to walk into and occupy a sculpture as opposed to merely admiring it as a static object from afar.

As the shapes have become more dramatic and moved once again from power symbols to city symbols, the role of the icon as a method for communication continues to evolve and shift. With the demise of the sculpture and the rise of the sculptural, these new examples of iconic architecture privilege sequence over spectacle and experience over legible symbolism. Rejecting Venturi's classifications of iconic architecture as either building as sign or building with sign, the projects appearing now, and featured in this book, engage an altogether different approach to symbolism. Less about identifying an image and more about experiencing it, these projects defy direct metaphorical categorization through the creation of a heightened emotional sensation. In exchange for the one-to-one translation of image into architectural form, this new manifestation of sculptural architecture proves more subtle in its approach, oscillating between representation and abstraction. Never settling on the purely legible or the purely lyrical, this tension represents the exact point where architecture becomes interesting again.

While the need for icons as communicative tools remains as strong as ever, the forms they come in no longer need to be clear symbols of familiar shapes. By prioritizing the creation of the new and surprising over the recognizable and literal, architects are now freer to experiment and innovate. Due to leaps in both technology and thought, no clear formula exists in terms of size, shape, material, or location for creating an architectural icon.

The development of a new language of sculptural architecture coincides with the emergence of new technologies, digital fabrication techniques, and computer power to inform and drive these contemporary shapes. As some still simply enlarge their hyperbolic dreams into an architectural scale, appearing like building-sized cardboard models, many more architects and designers choose to

new building typology that engages techniques of surrealism to produce an affective, immersive, and experiential approach to architecture. With forms becoming less legible and as a result more provocative, sheer size and ostentatious symbolism now play an increasingly marginal role in determining a building's impact. Instead, shape, form, texture, material, and spatial sequencing prove even more valuable and effective for generating meaningful and memorable spaces.

While the great skyscraper race has indeed enjoyed a resurgence since 2008, and will be showcased accordingly in the projects that follow, its revival also brings forth a whole new range of iconic structures that redefine the image of what can and should attract people to a city, town, village, and even the wild. By changing the demographics of architecture and finding new voices to express the different personalities and minds present within our global landscape, the profession and its body of work have become increasingly more pluralistic and diversified. From the exuberant, gravity-defying creations of Studio Fuksas, Jürgen Mayer, and UNStudio to the more understated work of Cor & Associates and Takeshi Hosaka, the dramatic range of projects featured in this book highlights the exceptional diversity developing within the sculptural architecture movement.

The resilience of iconic architecture derives its strength from its role within the human psyche. Mirroring the identity, personality, and cultural values of its surroundings, the anomaly plays a crucial, visceral, and psychological part in cultivating a person's connection to a place. In spite of the misappropriation of the icon for the benefit of big business and branding campaigns, the strength of the form speaks to its undeniable appeal in strengthening our relationship with the built environment and one another.

engage these emerging technologies to establish a new architectural vocabulary. Although both contrasting design approaches offer important contributions to the built environment, one camp explores the expressive potential of architecture in space, while the other advances the architectural field through the application of developing technologies in both design and construction.

For the icon to no longer be exclusively linked with symbols of power frees it from aesthetic constraints. Even so, a distinction remains between just another crazy form and a crazy form that has sculptural qualities. Instead of focusing on being larger, taller, and bigger, the contemporary interpretation of the iconic champions whim, personality, and play, appealing to our most basic emotions. Moving away from merely depicting a recognizable symbol to evoking pure, immersive sensation fuels instead a

1 Charles Jenks, "Part 2: Two Modes of Communication,"
in *The Language of Post-Modern Architecture* (1977), p. 39.
2 Robert Venture, Denise Scott Brown, Steven Izenour, "Part 1,"
in *Learning from Las Vegas* (1972), p. 12.

//ARTechnic Architects
Shell

//Massimiliano & Doriana Fuksas
Admirant Entrance Building

chapter 01
organic flow

//MAD
Ordos City Museum

//Zaha Hadid Architects
London Aquatics Center

//Paul Le Quernec & Michel Grasso
La Bulle Enchantée

At last, the type of expressive architecture that once seemed possible only in our wildest imagination is finally taking shape within our built reality. The rapid expansion of tools for design, engineering, and execution have ended the association of organic, undulating forms with exorbitant budgets and structural implausibility. Across the globe, new projects defy these structural constraints of the past. By investing in the development and application of new technological advancements in both the design and execution of buildings, what once limited the shape, size, and logic of a given form can now empower it.

Thanks to these breakthroughs in three-dimensional modeling, engineering, and digital fabrication techniques, buildings are able to manifest almost any shape. This freedom of form strengthens the role of organic structures within the sculptural architecture movement. From exploring new methods of casting concrete to treating interlocking pieces of wood as both structure and finished material, the sinuous shapes that follow offer breathtaking examples of current approaches to enhancing surface articulation, interior organization, and public interest.

The success of these organic shapes speaks to the power of architecture when it evokes a sense of the natural within the man-made. While these curving forms stand in dramatic contrast to their surrounding context and to the vast majority of their architectural predecessors, these confounding shapes are laced with something undeniably provocative and yet also extremely familiar. The use of the soft edge instead of the hard line inevitably creates a fluid dialogue between an organic structure and its natural surroundings. The crazier the curve, the more enticing it becomes for the viewer, inspiring symbolic and tactile connections to trees, plants, a mound of earth, or an entire landscape.

While the formal appearance of organic architecture grows increasingly more gestural and surprising, in the end, when applied at the scale of a building, even the craziest of forms needs to be instilled with functionality. From adding entrances and egresses to providing adequate circulation and daylighting, screws, bolts, mullions, seams, panels, apertures, walls, and floor plates comprise the main ingredients through which the vast majority of structures are derived. Able to take on more articulated shapes, this underlying structural logic makes it possible to execute any building, particularly an unusual one.

This same logic helps make these visually dazzling and somewhat alien forms recognizable and attractive to the general public, while also drawing a strong distinction between classical sculpture and sculptural architecture. As opposed to sculptures that typically begin with a single material (perhaps a block of granite or a large piece of wood), architecture cannot escape fragmentation due to its sheer size and scale. With this said, the inherent need and responsibility for architecture to combine a range of pieces and materials is exactly what makes the profession so interesting.

By utilizing these architectural elements to produce a practical solution that also emphasizes a fluidity of form, architects and designers can test the limits of complex curvature without losing the visceral qualities of the human touch. Exemplified in the revolutionary paneling techniques of Studio Fuksas in both their Admirant Entrance Building and Myzeil Shopping Mall, or in the supple concrete curves of Paul Le Quernec and Michel Grasso's enchanted kindergarten, the geometric ideal and the structural logic of these buildings inform one another, generating fantastical forms that remain rich in realism through their detailing. Jürgen Mayer's Metropol Parasol serves as another critical example of a design approach that pushes the limits of sculpted surfaces and construction methods simultaneously. By developing a framework of massive interlocking wooden elements that shift in size and shape, Mayer's surreal and undulating grid functions as both form and structure, exposing nothing and everything simultaneously. The masterful articulation of such dynamic surfaces through this evolving kit of parts enables these projects to function as successful urban muses ripe for the public imagination.

The bending, bulging, and voluptuous projects that sweep through the following pages capitalize on the increasing formal freedom generated by such breakthroughs in technology. These advances influence not only the construction process but also the design process, resulting in a myriad of enticing organic structures. By challenging preconceptions of what a building can look like and how it should be constructed, everything from expansive cultural centers to modest single-family homes can adopt and add to this new gestural formal language. The rise of these pliable and velvety shapes appeals to our curiosity, reinstating a sense of wonder with each new twist of the surface.

J. MAYER H. Architects
Metropol Parasol

Seville, Spain, 2011

A striking addition to the medieval inner city of Seville, this technologically groundbreaking project offers one of the largest and most innovative timber constructions in existence. The massive, undulating structure weaves across the plaza, providing shade and space for an archaeological museum, farmers market, and elevated plaza with a panorama terrace located at the very top of the parasols. Transforming an archaeological excavation site into a contemporary landmark, the project cultivates a unique relationship between the historical city and contemporary architecture.

Massimiliano & Doriana Fuksas
Myzeil Shopping Mall

Frankfurt, Germany, 2009

This surreal and expansive 6-floor shopping mall offers a visually and structurally complex portal between two important sites in the heart of Frankfurt. As if being pulled into the space by a vortex, the exterior façade sweeps through the project's interior, literally turning the building inside out. The mall achieves its undulating formal logic through a network of triangulated, reinforced glass panels. Illuminated by glowing, off-white edges, the building's interior swirls around the façade, blurring distinctions between inside and outside and challenging one's understanding of the laws of physics.

FREE Fernando Romero EnterprisE
Museo Soumaya

Mexico City, Mexico, 2011

Glittering like a sequin dress stretching up from the site, this iconic monolith functions as an art museum in an industrial section of Mexico City. The panelized façade is composed of a network of hexagonal aluminum tiles, resulting in a glistening and continuous exterior wrapper completely devoid of windows. As the building swells at the top, a cantilevered roof directs daylight into the six continuous levels of gallery space. Twenty-eight curving steel columns that vary in size and shape create the building's compellingly irregular form. This shining organic project gives an impressive new face and cultural beacon to the surrounding neighborhood.

Massimiliano & Doriana Fuksas
Admirant Entrance Building

Eindhoven, Netherlands, 2010

Part of an extensive master plan for central Eindhoven, this tessellated yet organic building serves as the new icon for the area. The amorphous object stands in stark contrast with its more conservative surroundings, bulging up from the ground like an undefined celestial body. The building shifts between white opaque triangular panels and maritime blue glass panels, which adds to its surreal visual composition. Keeping in line with the aesthetic of suddenly emerging from the ground or dropping in from outer space, the project has no front or back, which allows the exterior envelope to be experienced without interruption.

Foster + Partners
UAE Pavilion, Expo 2010 Shanghai

Shanghai, China, 2010

This prominent golden pavilion draws its inspiration from a sand dune, a symbolic feature of the desert landscape shared by each of the seven emirates. With a capacity of 450 people and enclosing 3,000 square meters of exhibition space, the pavilion stands as one of the largest structures built for the 2010 Shanghai Expo. The triangulated metallic surface reflects the sunlight, adding to the illusion of the building as an occupiable landscape. The fluid surfaces rise and fall, creating moments for fin-like apertures to appear, which direct light into the deepest corners of the interior.

Zaha Hadid Architects
London Aquatics Center

London, United Kingdom, 2011

Inspired by the fluid geometry of water in motion, this project will serve as the new aquatic center for the London 2012 Olympic Games. Reminiscent of a large wave, an undulating roof sweeps up from the ground to enclose the swimming and diving pools in a unifying gesture of fluidity. The double-curvature geometry of the ceiling creates a structure of parabolic arches that produces a visual separation between the competition pool space and the diving pool area. Cantilevered concrete diving boards rise from the ground at varying heights to create a dynamic visual composition and a professional space for aquatic sports and competition.

Studio Pei-Zhu
OCT Design Museum

Shenzhen, China, 2011

Just 300 meters from the ocean, this museum draws its
formal inspiration from the smooth stones found along
the beach. Set into its urban landscape, the building's
smooth, monolithic form appears to float just above
the ground, casting a surreal quality over the project.
The museum's interior directly reflects the exterior
form of the building in a single, continuous curving
space. This neutral yet transcendental white interior
casts no shadows and confounds one's ability to perceive depth within its borderless walls. Reminiscent of
being in a cloud or dense fog, the building becomes a
blank, ethereal background, punctuated only by a ran-
dom scattering of small, triangular windows.

Paul Le Quernec & Michel Grasso
La Bulle Enchantée

Sarreguemines, France, 2011

This softly curving nursery school provides an organic series of light-filled spaces that evoke a sense of safety and wonder. A large outdoor playground surrounds the central school area and offers privacy for the students through a curvilinear wall that also doubles as the perimeter of the facility. A pronounced concrete vault entrance blends into this peripheral wall, welcoming children and parents into the whimsical interior. The play areas radiate outward from the central nursery space and are connected by a continuous walkway that blurs one's sense of directionality within the school. The walls bend and seep into the interiors in rich hues, creating highly tactile and voluminous spaces that inspire the imagination in both children and adults alike.

MAD
Ordos City Museum

Ordos, China, 2011

Prominently perched atop the new center of Ordos, this iconic and organic museum contrasts with the strict linear geometry of the surrounding city's master plan. Enveloped in polished metal louvers, the bulging structure reflects and dissolves its rigid surroundings. The bronze-colored undulating mass lifts up to form an entrance, channeling visitors into a sumptuous white interior. The interior is divided into several exhibition halls defined by continuous curvilinear walls, all which open onto the shared public space that runs through the core of the museum. The glazed roof filters light into the building, which is then reflected between the luminescent walls. The bright, tranquil, and fluid environment of this project offers visitors a compelling environment to experience their culture, as well as a memorable beacon for their new city.

UNStudio
MUMUTH House for Music and Music Theater

Graz, Austria, 2008

Adding a twist to the classical relationship between music and architecture, this expressive music school offers an inspiring space for study and practice. A large spiral winds through the interior, splitting into a number of interconnected smaller spirals that organically divide the building and create a sense of directionality between the spaces. A fluid internal spatial arrangement efficiently links the rooms together. The free-flowing foyer boasts a massive twisting concrete staircase that connects the three levels of the building and doubles as a central design feature of the public space. The comparatively understated exterior comprises a glittering mesh wrapper that varies in density and transparency, sheltering the vibrant interior from public view.

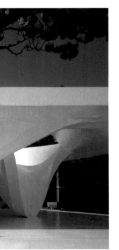

UNStudio
Burnham Pavilion

Chicago, Illinois, USA, 2009

This project stood as one of two temporary architectural pavilions built in Millennium Park to commemorate the 100th anniversary of the Plan of Chicago, making a bold visual statement about the city's ambitious, forward-thinking spirit. The floating roof, connected to the ground plane by three sinuous folds in the surface, offered surprising views of the Chicago skyline. Completely recyclable, this gleaming white pavilion was produced locally and built from donated steel and aluminum. The highly accessible sculptural pavilion served as an effective urban activator for the area. Programmatically, the pavilion invited people to gather, walk around and through the space, and explore and observe their surroundings. Framed by Lake Michigan on one side and Michigan Avenue on the other, the stunning pavilion related to and enhanced the diverse city contexts, programs, and scales.

Estudio Barozzi Veiga
//Fabrizio Barozzi, Alberto Veiga
Auditorium and Congress Palace Infanta Doña Elena in Águilas

Águilas, Spain, 2011

The project carefully mediates between the particularities of its urban site and the expressive nature of its concave façades. Defining and articulating these aesthetic contrasts allows the project to be organized independently while presenting a coherent response to the constraints dictated by its oceanfront location. The striking yet understated white volume directly reflects its surrounding context, becoming clean and orderly when facing the town and more playful and formally expressive while tangent to the sea.

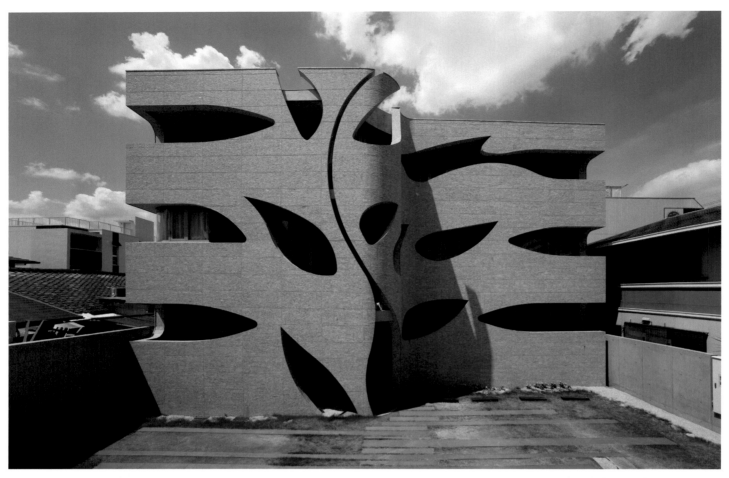

Eastern Design Office
//Anna Nakamura & Taiyo Jinno
Villa Saitan

Kyoto, Japan, 2006

This 11-unit housing complex rejects the conventional aesthetic of a typical apartment block by presenting itself as a single large house. Instead of a façade that differentiates each individual apartment, the design wraps the exterior with a thick wall of concrete. This prominent wrapper unifies the disparate apartments into a visually cohesive architectural expression. Playful apertures inspired by nature pierce through this heavy façade to generate unique entry points, balconies, skylights, and windows for the apartments.

Rudy Ricciotti
Jean Cocteau Museum
Menton, France, 2011

This monolithic shell serves as a comprehensive museum dedicated to the French artist and writer Jean Cocteau. A transparent glass box housing the main exhibition space nestles within a massive white concrete wrapper. The edges of this exterior volume are incrementally carved away to form windows, skylights, and entrances to the building. These irregular cutouts instill the museum with an organic and graphic visual quality and cultivate a feeling of movement and lightness within an otherwise overwhelming building mass.

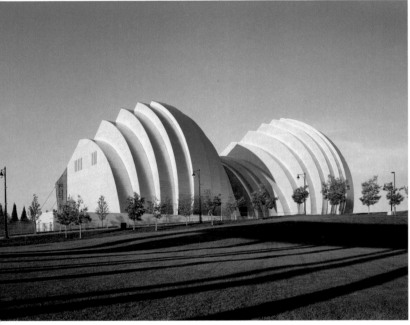

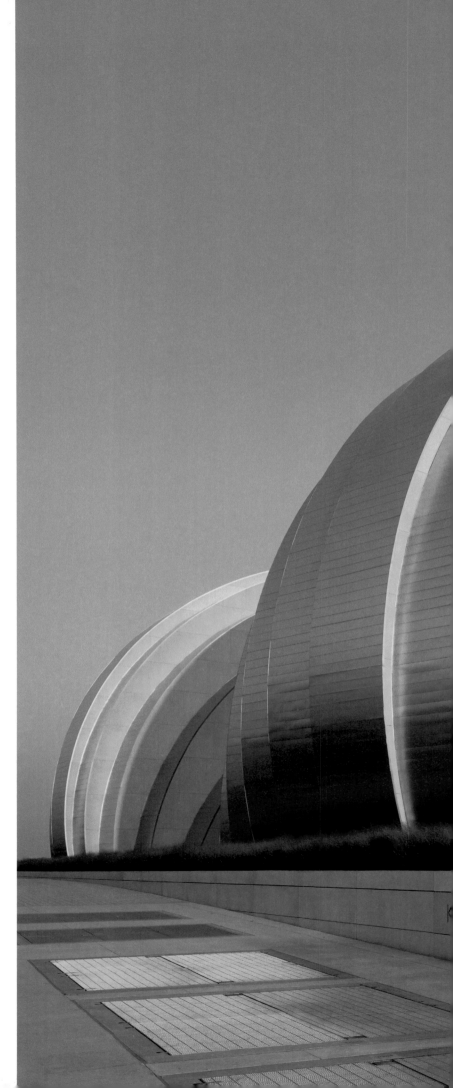

Safdie Architects
Kauffman Center for the Performing Arts

Kansas City, Missouri, USA, 2011

An undulating structure comprised of oversized, vertical segments of a circle houses a proscenium theater, concert hall, and banquet hall. These massive structural elements rise and fall, creating the illusion of a building in constant motion. The shell-like form swells in height on each side to accommodate the performance spaces, and dips in toward the center of the building to offer a more personal and intimate entry area. The south side of the building boasts an expansive, inclined curtain wall over the foyers that links the main auditoriums, flooding this transitional space with daylight and impressive views to the outdoors.

CENTER FOR THE PERFORMING ARTS

//Safdie Architects
Kauffman Center for the Performing Arts

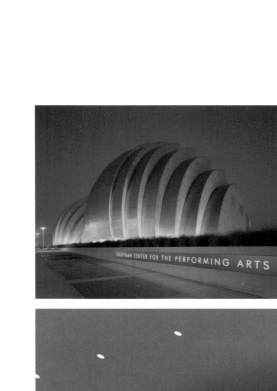

Studio Nicoletti Associati & Hijjas Kasturi Associates sdn
The Pod Exhibition Hall

Kuala Lumpur, Malaysia, 2011

Just west of Kuala Lumpur stands this iconic striated pavilion. Inspired by the formal logic of water droplets, this project consists of a series of elliptical sections stacked together that vary in width and height. Gaps between these segments allow for the placement of windows to bring natural daylight into the spaces. The hall appears to be sliced diagonally into a series of ribbons which wrap up and over the building to create a dynamic and layered protective shell. The structure is fabricated from tubular steel members with the exterior skin made of spectrally reflective aluminum panels. The color of this exterior skin changes depending on the reflection of the sun.

Ciel Rouge Création
//Henri Gueydan
Villa Ronde

Japan, 2010

A former hill turned seaside residence and private museum, this building without corners lets the strong winds of the coast optimize its design. The rounded façades bring light and panoramic views into the building through elliptical apertures that shift in scale. A central courtyard receives the southern light and distributes it throughout the interior. Evoking the classical language of an old fortress by the sea, the circle disappears into the cliff while still functioning as a panoramic tower for those inside. The circular floor plan allows for fluid circulation, as all rooms are connected, wrapping around the main internal courtyard. Seamlessly integrating with the surrounding nature, the landscape moves up and over the building, creating a lush garden rooftop for enjoying the sea.

ARTechnic Architects
//Kotaro Ide
Shell

Nagano, Japan, 2008

Nestled in the woods of a mountain resort town north-west of Tokyo, this house consists of two truncated oval masses of different size. These concrete cylinders act as thick shells, enveloping the interior spaces in a single fluid gesture. Coexisting with the natural surroundings, the design of the two shells are informed by the extant fir trees and landscape. With the terraces and windows wrapped around the natural highlights of the site, the project provides adequate shelter from and connection to the picturesque outdoors.

Becker Architekten
Hydroelectric Power Station

Kempten, Germany, 2010

This curving concrete form serves as a highly efficient hydroelectric power station, replacing an outdated version from the 1950s. The design concept comprises a continuous concrete wrapping that reaches between the two banks of the river. Part emerged and part submerged, the underground construction uses a concrete shell reinforced with a prominent ribbing system. This structural skeleton generates an impressive sequence of interior rooms that vary in scale from massive to intimate. The interior lighting percolates through gaps in the exterior shell, illuminating the arched passages. Implementing practical technology inside an expressive form results in a state of the art power station that simultaneously establishes a compelling new image for the city.

Stéphane Maupin
RATP Formation Center

Paris, France, 2010

Situated on the outskirts of Paris and surrounded by highways, train tracks, factories, and social housing complexes, this unusual project derives its formal inspiration from the raw atmosphere of its context. Designed as the headquarters for Parisian train workers, the simple 22-meter-high extrusion appears like a triangular wedge of concrete cake planted into the industrial site. Playful circular windows of varying sizes perforate this concrete shell, adding a touch of whimsy to the imposing façade. The combination of washbasin, soap dispenser, and colorized mirror in the locker room replicates the appearance of a smiling face, resulting in a welcoming and amusing space for employees to unwind.

1024 Architecture
1UP Mushroom

Saint-Denis, France, 2011

Finding its name and formal inspiration from the colorful mushrooms of Super Mario Bros., this whimsically imposing project operates as an archaeological education center. The project functions as a stylistic and programmatic hybrid between two cultures and generations, hosting a twelfth-century building inside a contemporary red and white hat. This cheerful and monolithic mushroom infuses the archaeological site with new life, making it an accessible public place for children and archeology students to learn and experiment.

Conix Architects
Facelift Umicore

Antwerp, Belgium, 2009

This striking project serves as part of a master plan to establish a vibrant new corporate identity on the site, and achieves this improved feeling through a singular, fluid move. Beginning at the entrance and culminating in the administrative area, which serves as the heart of the site, the bold intervention consists of one large folded zinc plate. This central office building contrasts with its monotonous urban surroundings, inspiring an impressive visual response that counters the existing rational background. The powerful look and feel of this undulating wrapped structure inspires an innovative image that modernizes the company and its site simultaneously.

J. MAYER H. Architects
Sarpi Border Checkpoint
Sarpi, Georgia, 2011

Located on the shore of the Black Sea, this graphic customs checkpoint greets visitors as they cross the Georgian border into Turkey. With its cantilevering terraces, the tower functions as a viewing platform with multiple levels overlooking the water and the steep coastline. The building confounds the eye with its hyper-flat yet wiggling form. As if the building were simply extruded from a sketch on a piece of paper, the building's flamboyantly expressive cantilevered form defies contemporary approaches to structural engineering and space planning. This iconic, yet undeniably surreal checkpoint welcomes visitors to Georgia, representing both the progressive upsurge of the country and the architectural mind.

//BNKR Arquitectura
Sunset Chapel

//Barbosa & Guimarães
Oporto Vodafone Building

chapter 02
sharp **structures**

//Preston Scott Cohen
Herta and Paul Amir Building,
Tel Aviv Museum of Art

//Toyo Ito & Associates, Architects
Toyo Ito Museum of Architecture,
Imabari

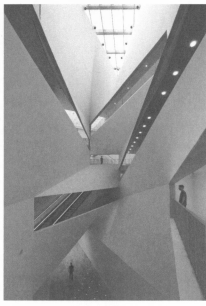

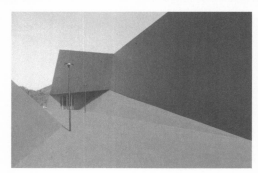

//Enota
Podčetrtek Sports Hall

The definition and accentuation of the edge and the corner offer sensational opportunities for enhancing architectural geometries. As architecture moves away from the literal and toward the figural and gestural, new techniques in surface articulation are emerging. Building on the monolithic forms made famous by the fascist and brutalist periods, these structures simultaneously evoke the sophisticated language of a bunker and a precious gem.

Such crystalized and expressive forms serve as yet another example of the power of technological advancements to inform and improve architectural design. What once was a massive, undefined monument can now gain added aesthetic value and depth through the sharpening and fracturing of its lines. Developments in panelizing, structural framing, and complex curvature instill within these imposing forms another level of detail that complements the greater formal gesture.

The shift away from the typical box and toward a more compelling architectural expression results in the appearance of angular projects that use the same underlying building logic to achieve something entirely different. By taking the static box and folding, creasing, faceting, chamfering, edging, and dividing it, these projects successfully activate each of its six sides. The treatment of four walls, a roof, and a ground plane as a critical and integrated single surface produces buildings that convey a sense of movement and dynamism without the use of a single curved line.

Unlike super smooth surfaces that often lack a discernible proportion and size, the projects that follow automatically define a clear sense of scale through their prominent creases and edges. Standing in opposition to the typical block as a medium, these angular borders strategically articulate a surface, as opposed to merely repeating an already too familiar silhouette. Shaking off the preconceptions of what a building composed of straight lines should look like, these futuristic forms prove just as effective and sculptural as the flowing, organic surfaces seen in the previous chapter.

A great visual strength and weight exudes from the tactile tessellations of these origami-inspired buildings. Rem Koolhaas's architecture office, OMA, initiated a similar formal exploration into the world of low-resolution shapes by translating a car and a series of other non-linear, complex forms into pixelated versions of themselves. While simplified to only the most rudimentary angles, this experiment remains compelling and relevant due to how much detail and information can still be expressed through the use of just a few smartly placed lines.

The more faceted the project, the more visual drama ensues. These edgy forms become less focused on gradients, instead producing a high-contrast aesthetic driven by the intensity of the shadows present within their underlying angled geometry. Exemplified by Preston Scott Cohen's Tel Aviv Museum of Art and Clavel Arquitectos' Cloud Pantheon, such an attitude toward form-making cultivates a fractal image, rich in granularity and emotional impact.

This turbulent yet rhythmic approach to sculptural architecture retains a closer relationship to more traditional styles of architecture than one might initially imagine. These same angular qualities can be traced back to the motif of the church, not just in the presence of its stained glass imagery but also in the unusually slanted shape of the bell tower. The ability to evoke both the sacred and ethereal through heavy, inclined masses stands as the underlying effect that makes these geometric forms so provocative and powerful.

The innate formal logic of such a pronounced building typology requires the architect to approach its structure and shape within the same gesture. Differing from typical iconic, flowing surfaces, where image comes first and all of the technical aspects are dealt with later or never fully resolved, the language of these idiosyncratic structures remains tethered to and supported by the requirements of their structure and context. Never escaping the pragmatic realities involved when translating design from paper into actual building, this style of architecture is already conceived in terms of panels, steps, seams, and framing. The articulation that occurs not only establishes a sequence of directions in the surface, but can also reduce or heighten the visual density of the form based on the number of folds, pleats, or borders it applies. The assertive and muscular forms appearing in this chapter create a sense of weight, attitude, and density, evoking a feeling of the sublime that transcends each project's size and function.

56

Lyons
John Curtin School of Medical Research Stage 1, The Australian National University

Canberra, Australia, 2006

Appearing as a great retractable shell reaching toward the street, this angular structure serves as one of Australia's leading biomedical research institutes. The low-rise building is connected through a series of origami-style folded segments that promotes interaction between staff, researchers, and visitors. Using strands of DNA as aesthetic inspiration, the exterior façade of the building expresses the work undertaken by the school through its form and surface texture. Two aluminum strands at the top and bottom of the façade wind continuously around the building, twisting into a three-dimensional version of a double helix at the entrance. The foyer walls are composed of aluminum-clad fins inset with full-height tinted glass. The project challenges the conventional paradigm of an enclosed research institute, instead delivering an open and adaptive laboratory and office environment.

Clavel Arquitectos
//Manuel Clavel Rojo
Cloud Pantheon
Murcia, Spain, 2010

A seemingly demure box from the outside and an otherworldly example of faceted surface articulation from within, this project draws its formal inspiration from the mysterious transition between life and death. Oversized angular doors merge together to obscure the entrance to the building. Once inside, visitors are greeted by an impressive white articulated mass streaked with light. This complex form captures an element of the sublime, as it overwhelms the senses with its size, precarious complexity, and undeniably ethereal aesthetic qualities.

//Clavel Arquitectos
Cloud Pantheon

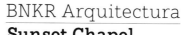

BNKR Arquitectura
Sunset Chapel

Acapulco, Mexico, 2011

This bunker-like concrete chapel disguises itself as a colossal boulder perched atop a mountain. Angled to take advantage of the spectacular views of the bay, the sun sets exactly behind the altar cross. A space to both celebrate marriage and honor the dead, this project plays with juxtapositions of material and shape to create a form in constant dialogue with itself and its somewhat contradictory functions. By contrasting glass with concrete, transparency with solidity, and classical proportions with contemporary articulation, this striking chapel creates an ethereal yet seemingly indestructible space for reflection.

TEL AVIV MUSEUM OF ART מוזיאון תל אביב לאמנות
HERTA & PAUL AMIR BUILDING הבניין ע"ש שמואל והרטה עמיר

Preston Scott Cohen
Herta and Paul Amir Building, Tel Aviv Museum of Art

Tel Aviv, Israel, 2011

This building represents an unusual synthesis of two opposing paradigms for the contemporary museum: the museum as a series of neutral white boxes and the museum as an architectural spectacle. Located on a narrow, triangular site, the subtly twisting geometric surfaces connect the disparate angles between the galleries and the site, while refracting natural light into the deepest recesses of the half-buried building. These individual, rectangular galleries are organized around an 87-foot-tall spiraling atrium. Both beacon and monolith, the formally complex and faceted museum emphasizes its connection to contemporary architecture and the culturally and historically rich fabric of Tel Aviv.

//Preston Scott Cohen
Herta and Paul Amir Building,
Tel Aviv Museum of Art

Barbosa & Guimarães
//José António Barbosa & Pedro Lopes Guimarães
Oporto Vodafone Building

Porto, Portugal, 2009

This tessellated office building conveys a sense of movement as it winds its way around a busy city corner. Designed using a linear approach, the building begins to pinch and pull, becoming an irregular body that challenges the static nature of the built environment. The concrete façade creates irregular and free-form shapes, working as a structural solution that creates a unique yet monolithic building. The crystalline exterior extends through the interior with faceted white corridors illuminated by crisscrossing skylights that run across the space.

Schmidhuber + Partner
German Pavilion, Expo 2010 Shanghai

Shanghai, China, 2010

This precariously sculpted form hovers between instability and balance. When considered as a whole, the various angled forms appear to hold each other in perfect equilibrium. Cantilevered polygonal elements create levitating exhibition spaces and landscapes that interlace with the interior. The façade of the pavilion is covered by a transparent textile skin. This silver fabric, with its subtle glow, allows for a constant connection between interior and exterior while offering shade and reflecting up to 80 percent of the solar radiation. The architecture integrates innovative and intelligent materials to create a building that doubles as a walk-through sculpture.

Heri & Salli
Hausplatz Jordan

Klagenfurt, Austria, 2008

This angular and adjustable poolside lounge serves as a highly efficient and striking extension to an existing traditional single-family house. Fabricated from six large white panels that can fold and bend, the space remains in a state of constant flux as it adjusts to the needs of its users. Flipping up or down to become walls, ceilings, floors, tables, or lounge chairs, these modular plates produce a visually dramatic geometric composition while achieving maximum utility. The panels along the edges of the lounge extend out into the pool area, creating a seamless transition between enclosure and walkway.

left page
DW5 & Bernard Khoury Architects
Plot 7950—Sfeir Residence

Faqra, Lebanon, 2010

Located on a steep site in the hills of Mount Lebanon, this unusual residence spreads over three levels down the sloping plot. The frontal façade, located on the upper edge of the site, maintains a discreet cylindrical profile that emerges from the ground and wraps around the building, extending all the way to the edge of the plot 10 meters below. An intermediary level above the base accommodates two guest suites and a gym with fully openable glazing and direct access to a sundeck terrace and lap pool. The main reception hall and dining area enjoy maximum exposure to the preferred views and access to a large outdoor balcony. The balcony also serves as an open air elevator platform that connects the reception floor to the terrace below. Two master suites are located on the upper level and are covered by a retractable vault, providing the owners with the option to sleep under the stars.

this page
Plot 4238

Kfardebian, Lebanon, 2010

Located on a tight parcel atop steep topography, the south façade of this project connects to the access road through an inclined plateau that starts at ground level and slopes up seven meters in the northern direction. The inclined surface acts as both roof and oblique street façade, stepping up to an elevated pool at the northern tip of the slope. The angled plane also leads visitors up to the mid-level main entrances located on the eastern and western edges of the roof. The north façade is glazed from floor to ceiling, and provides long and narrow balconies with spectacular views of the valley. The east and west sides have limited openings that enable access to intermediate terraces and produce a shifting checkered pattern along the main façade. The two interiors are organized on three levels with reception spaces located on the upper floor. The northern terraces of the project are accessible from the interior via a mobile balcony that travels vertically along the façade.

Metaform Architecture
Apartment Building

Luxembourg City, Luxembourg, 2011

The monolithic character of this building stands in stark contrast to its neighbors, differing from them in both form and construction materials. The project appears as a unique and independent object, characterized by the shifted stacking of a repetitive volume. By using a single material, in this case a shiny black metal, the project develops an imposing presence, taking on the character of a slumbering animal. The shifted rectangular layers create space for terraces above and for playful and colorful illustrations below. The result of a collaboration between artist and architect, these bright orange and red surfaces enhance the theatricality of the project, adding a bit of whim and saturation to the rigid form. The panelized façade allows the building to be both public and private, as it opens and closes based on the needs of those inside.

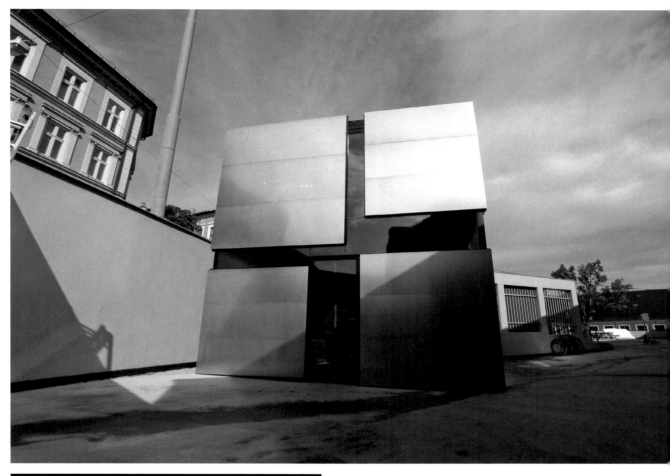

Rintala Eggertsson Architects
Box Home

Oslo, Norway, 2007

For a compact house, this project leaves a big impression. The 19-square-meter dwelling consists of four rooms that cover all basic living functions from dining to resting. Focusing on enhancing the quality of space, material, and natural light, the house reduces any unnecessary floor area. This home serves as a dwelling prototype that can be expanded to accommodate larger family housing or even an office setting. Such a stealth, urban cave offers respite and shelter from the intensity of the surrounding city.

A-cero, Joaquín Torres Architects
1001 Nights House

Madrid, Spain, 2011

Resembling an arched bunker, this massive single-family home serves as a granite-clad fortress for relaxation and leisure. The imposing house sprawls atop a 7,000-square-meter site yet remains well-hidden by a series of curved walls that rise up from the adjacent pools of water surrounding the entrance. A wide stone path flanked by these shallow water elements leads to an enormous black glass door that provides access to the interior. The private rear façade of the house remains extremely open compared to the front entrance and includes a wide porch, pool, garden, and lounge area. All rooms face out onto this expansive backyard area and enjoy large windows that encourage a strong connection to the outdoors, even within such a well-protected stone enclosure.

this page
A.L.X. (Architect Label Xain) //Junichi Sampei
Dancing Living House

Yokohama, Japan, 2008

This striking white mass doubles as both a private residence and dance studio for a Japanese couple. Clad in a thick concrete to buffer sound, the building's exterior is treated as a single, unified element. The pristine cube lifts up at its base to accommodate parking for two cars and an entry to the dance studio. The main house hovers above the studio and integrates strips of glass along the floor to channel light into the studio below. By acting as both floor and skylight, this technique allows the façade to remain free of windows, establishing a sense of privacy and intimacy for the dancers.

right page
On the Cherry Blossom

Tokyo, Japan, 2008

Facing two cherry trees on a narrow corner lot, this unusual cubic home, much like a tree, grows and expands first vertically and then horizontally. The graphic white composition functions a bit like a reverse setback, beginning with a single entry cube and increasing in complexity and size the higher it goes. Skylights and small window slits capture light for the lower levels and promote ventilation. The main living spaces are concentrated on the top and largest floor to enjoy the prime view of the cherry trees and instill a connection to nature.

Office of Ryue Nishizawa
Garden & House

Tokyo, Japan, 2011

Squeezed into a high-density Tokyo neighborhood on a narrow 32-square-meter site, this unusual stacked home provides a series of spaces that blur the distinction between interior and exterior. The project offers a refreshing combination of offices, private dormitories and living spaces, and gardens. The structure consists of a vertical layer of horizontal slabs that create a building without walls, bringing in light to the dark site and promoting ventilation. Each room is paired with a corresponding garden, providing a sense of openness and connection to the outdoors. With each room smaller than its floor slab, the layout allows for freedom in determining the relationship between room and garden, regardless of the floor level.

Ikimono Architects
//Takashi Fujino
Static Quarry

Gunma, Japan, 2011

As if excavated from a giant block of concrete, these unusual housing units produce a dramatic juxtaposition between solid and void. Aligned and interlocking courtyards allow for an unobstructed visual path through the 8-unit complex from the street, promoting a sense of transparency and openness within the imposing mass. The building's density operates like a small city, promoting interaction between neighbors. Each dwelling faces onto the main courtyard, connecting the residents to the outdoors and one another.

Yasutaka Yoshimura Architects
Nowhere but Sajima
Yokosuka, Japan, 2009

This austere weekly vacation house serves as part of a designer resort program along the Japanese coast. Comprised of a plain white cube, the project gains its character and interest through its highly expressive and diagrammatic window shapes. As if punched into the façade by an array of cookie cutters and then extruded into the space, these geometric apertures vary from oversized rectangle to house-shaped silhouette and truncated oval. With no two windows alike, each unit overlooks the ocean through its own unique frame.

Carmody Groarke
Studio East Dining

London, United Kingdom, 2010

Built on top of a 35-meter-high multistory car park, this temporary restaurant pavilion enjoyed elevated views across London's 2012 Olympic site. Comprised of a series of interlocking white rectangles with large glass openings at each end for key rooftop views, the space contained an expansive dining room which allowed up to 140 guests to be connected in a single, communal dining experience. The project was designed and built within ten weeks and had a life span of only three weeks. Constructed with hired materials borrowed from the existing, surrounding construction site, the building components were returned at the end of the project.

89

Herzog & de Meuron
VitraHouse

Weil am Rhein, Switzerland, 2010

This surreal museum reinvents the theme of the archetypal house by treating it as a stacked volume. Due to its exposed location and striking appearance, the project assumes the important role of marking the Vitra Campus. Showcasing designed home furnishings, the 5-story form nurtures a legibility and connection to its interior function. The proportions and dimensions of the interior spaces lend the project a domestic scale reminiscent of familiar residential settings. The individual cantilevering houses are conceived as abstract elements, with large glazed faces displaying the items within. A chaotic yet organized pile of 12 intersecting houses, the project creates a three-dimensional assemblage that glows across the surrounding landscape.

SelgasCano
//Jose Selgas & Lucia Cano
Merida Factory Youth Movement

Merida, Spain, 2011

Conceived as a large canopy open to the city, this colorful and angular project serves as a dynamic, multipurpose space for recreation. Supported by a series of muscular glowing modules that house internal programs, the expansive canopy protects visitors from the rain and sun. The undulating, translucent roof extends like a light cloud over the center. Constructed from a three-dimensional mesh structure, the tessellated canopy flattens into a vertical climbing wall on one side, bridging the gap between floor and ceiling.

Tomás García Píriz/ CUAC Arquitectura with Jose L. Muñoz
Biodiversity Center

Loja, Spain, 2011

Emerging from a sloping site, this angular project embeds itself into the landscape and bends to accommodate an existing tree on the plot. The stealth white mass sharply contrasts with its natural surroundings. With one side of the building almost entirely buried, large slits cut from the geometry direct light into the space and frame key views by promoting a strong visual connection between interior and exterior. The clean lines of the exterior façade combined with the bright modernist aesthetic of the interior set up a dynamic and compelling tension between architecture and nature.

Enota
Podčetrtek Sports Hall

Podčetrtek, Slovenia, 2010

This monolithic municipal sports hall stands in stark contrast to the local architectural vernacular. An angled "red carpet" of sorts welcomes visitors to the hall and leads them to the main entrance. This hyper-flat graphic walkway is cut from the existing earth bank and folds up on each side, creating a sense of outdoor enclosure and providing a visual accent to the massive black building. Finished in a vivid red, the angled path widens before reaching the entrance. The building's perforated black cladding remains hidden during the day, only revealing its abstracted floral patterns at night. With one look by day and another by night, this two-faced project functions as a dramatic aesthetic beacon for the community.

Toyo Ito & Associates, Architects
Toyo Ito Museum of Architecture, Imabari

Imabari, Japan, 2011

Built on a hilly site overlooking the Seto Inland Sea, this angular museum consists of two hyper-geometric buildings for exhibition and workshop activities. The building forms stand in stark contrast to the surrounding landscape and emerge out of four types of polyhedron modules, which can be freely assembled and closely packed. Each unit has two kinds of wall slant angles that blur definite distinctions between ceilings, walls, and floors. As visitors move from one room to another, the inclined walls unfold panoramically. This unique quality of the space enables unusual ways of exhibiting work completely different from an orthodox exhibition space based upon a standard grid.

//Matsys
P_Wall

//Studio Gang Architects
Aqua Tower

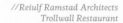

chapter 03
smarter surface

//Cor & Asociados
Music Hall and Auditorium
in Algueña MUCA

//Reiulf Ramstad Architects
Trollwall Restaurant

//Kengo Kuma & Associates
GC Prostho Museum Research Center

Much like the face of a person, the façade of a building represents the first, and sometimes only, impression that can be offered to the outside world. In terms of successful branding and marketing, whether a building proves memorable or instantly forgettable relies almost exclusively on its exterior image. The image or character that these structures project to the public becomes their corporate and cultural identity. Based on which exterior wrapper it chooses to wear, the façade establishes a unique image that sells a given brand, or rather its building, through calculated architectural expression.

Acting as the main, and most obvious element of a building, the façade communicates both an address and identity. Beginning with the naming of buildings and towers to generate interest and develop a recognizable landmark within the city, the focus has now shifted instead to the enhancement of their forms. Aided in part by the propagation of GPS programs that map our urban areas through photos taken from both street and aerial view, the architectural exterior proves more vulnerable to aesthetic scrutiny than ever before. Utilizing new techniques to achieve this lucrative razzle dazzle effect, buildings are becoming less about name and size and more about image and articulation.

The role of the façade serves both aesthetic and pragmatic functions. A building's exterior shell operates as the visual and experiential interface between the city and the interior of the building. Nevertheless, the façade also comprises one of the most crucial and inherently functional parts of a building: the skin. This external wrapper distinguishes a building from a tent, outdoor pavilion, or other temporary structure. As the main function of the building is to provide shelter from the outside and protect against shifts in climate, only after the façade achieves this shielding quality can it focus on the cosmetics.

A successful façade finds a way to synthesize and balance shelter on the one hand and aesthetics on the other. This dual role of the façade references back to the first chapter on organic architecture through its combination of sculptural gesture with a functional need and requirement. While the façade provides a certain identity to the outside world, it still must achieve a range of requirements within. From bringing in a certain amount of natural daylight and ventilation to enabling proper circulation, the responsibility of the façade constantly mediates between offering an aesthetic and sculptural experience and meeting basic needs in terms of use. However, such a fluid integration of both form and function results in new and exciting possibilities for the façade.

As the role of the façade continues to evolve, developing yet another sparkling skin is no longer enough. With the trend of treating the façade as mere superficial packaging finally falling out of style, in its place appears a new generation of projects that approach a building as a continuous, unified expression from inside to out. While the role of the exterior still offers great opportunities for formulating a message and defining an address, architects are finally capitalizing on the spatial and experiential opportunities that reflect the inside on the outside (and vice versa).

Providing clues as to what awaits visitors on the inside adds heightened value and aesthetic intrigue to a project. Not only does such a comprehensive design approach attract the greater community to come in and explore the interior, but it also works the other way around to connect the building's users to their surroundings. By linking the exterior to the interior, the façade behaves as a giant interface or membrane, constantly mediating and permeating between the built and surrounding environment.

Becoming more than just beautiful sculptures, masks, and wrappers, the contemporary façade proves increasingly more versatile at establishing a fluid aesthetic dialogue that engages all parts of a building and its context. From the whimsically surreal Hotel Inntel Zaandam by WAM Architecten, which uses the classical building vernacular of the Dutch cottage to create something entirely contemporary, to the undulating Aqua Tower by Studio Gang that challenges the aesthetics of the skyscraper, the diverse projects that follow showcase the exceptional range of scales, sizes, and approaches that a façade can manifest. By trading in the superficial for the experiential, the versatility and importance of the façade become more than just skin deep.

The façade serves as one of the few transforming elements of a building. Able to change from day to night but also throughout the seasons, the color, texture, transparency, and atmosphere of this exterior skin enjoy a tremendous amount of aesthetic freedom. These shifting effects add a sense of vibrancy and dynamism to a project, as if the building might in fact be a living and breathing organism. The projects that follow demonstrate the innovative and diverse design possibilities that arise when the façade is treated less as a static cover and more as a spatial experience that can enhance both the image of our buildings as well as our cities.

WAM Architecten
//Wilfried van Winden
Hotel Inntel Zaandam

Zaandam, Netherlands, 2010

Inspired by the green wooden houses of the Zaan region, this iconic hotel consists of a whimsical stacking of nearly 70 examples of these traditional houses, ranging from a notary's residence to a worker's cottage. Located in the center of the city, the 11-floor tower is painted in four shades of green that are native to the region, adding an aura of familiarity to the strikingly idiosyncratic design. Linking present and past with tradition and innovation, this uncanny project transcends and reinvigorates the local aesthetic while developing a design sensibility with universal appeal.

103

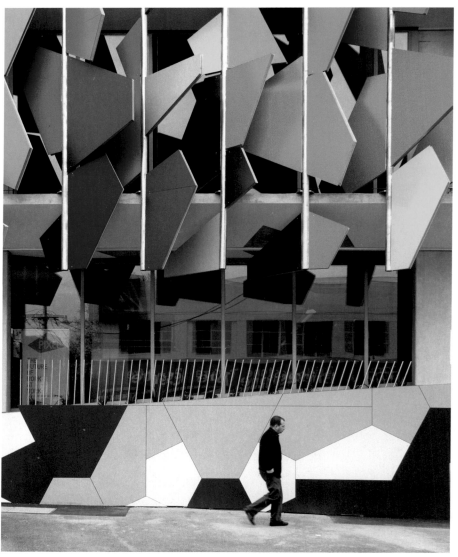

studio505
Pixel

Melbourne, Australia, 2010

This eye-catching project stands as Australia's first carbon-neutral office building. The exuberant and layered façade comprises a simple but intricate assembly of zero-waste, recycled color panels. Each geometric panel is slightly different, providing unique daylight, shade, and views for the interior spaces. The façade wraps continuously around the building, adding a vibrant and unique identity to the neighborhood. As if the building trapped a swarm of exotic butterflies, the tactile and angular façade conveys a sense of playful motion.

ACXT
//Javier Pérez Uribarri &
Nicolás Espinosa Barrientos
Bilbao Arena and Sports Center

Bilbao, Spain, 2010

Built on ancient iron mines adjacent to the old part of town, this elevated arena and sports center doubles as both a professional events hall and an activity center for the general public. A panelized façade of different shades of green wraps the main arena and circulation corridors, providing a striking visual identity evocative of a large tree canopy hovering above a series of white trunks. Certain panels are left out of the façade to provide sweeping city views and promote ventilation. An indoor arena and pool complement the building's exterior aesthetic through a playful integration of greens, yellows, and whites into the general color scheme.

Wingårdh Arkitektkontor //Gert Wingårdh & Jonas Edblad

Kuggen

Gothenburg, Sweden, 2011

This distinctive cylindrical building in the middle of the town square serves as a playful red icon for the city. The round form offers an impressive amount of floor space in relation to the amount of exposed exterior wall surface. The upper floors project out over the lower levels to create a building that partially protects itself from the sun. A rotating mesh screen provides additional shading for the top floors, following the sun's path around the building. The triangular-shaped windows establish a graphic identity for the project while maximizing light intake to the interior. The brocade of red-glazed terra cotta panels reflects in the light, enhancing the building's evolving appearance throughout the day.

Manuelle Gautrand
Architecture
La Cite Des Affaires

Saint-Etienne, France, 2010

Rising like a large Aztec serpent, this project functions as a vital liaison between the city center and surrounding neighborhoods. The complex rears up and unfolds to form an easily accessible building with open, spacious courtyards and bold overhangs. The highly flexible project also serves as a prominent urban landmark. Forming a continuous surface, the building's façade comprises two contrasting yet complementary stylistic approaches. While its bulk is wrapped in a silvery skin of transparent glazing, the main faces are painted in a cheerful canary yellow. These yellow planes shift between floating canopy and vertical wall, accompanying pedestrian movements with their rich, luminous presence. The nearness of such a vivid color brightens up the pavement and glazed elevations, casting golden washes over them like sunlight.

Ateliers Jean Nouvel
100 11th Avenue
New York, USA, 2010

Neighboring an angular Frank Gehry complex, this softly rounded residential tower proves eye-catching in its own right. The main façade along the waterfront encases the building's tallest point at 21 floors. An architectural rendition of an impressionist painting, the façade comprises a network of rectangular pieces of blue and green glass that vary in size to create a glistening canvas, capturing the nuanced way light reflects off water. Playing with its proximity to the river and its own reflection, the complexity of the project results in a camouflaged icon, visually prominent yet somehow invisible.

111

Manuelle Gautrand
Architecture
C_42: Citroën Flagship Showroom

Paris, France, 2007

This prismatic façade project covers a classic rectangular building from the 1920s. Keeping with the minimalist yet contemporary approach of the original building, the new façade begins at street level with the application of a large row of glazed rectangles tinted a classic Citroën red. Higher up the building, a series of large chevron panels appear, giving the project a crystalized origami aesthetic. The articulation of the façade maintains an inverse relationship to the entry level, increasing in three-dimensionality the higher up it goes. Inspired by the design logic of the cars it sells, the building becomes a molded, fluid surface that links the front, roof, and rear, establishing a perfect unity between place and product.

Manuelle Gautrand
Architecture
Origami Building

Paris, France, 2011

Inspired by the logic of origami, an array of shifting tri-angulated panels comprise the dynamic façade of this intriguing office building. These translucent, three-dimensional panels are removed at different intervals to bring daylight directly into the interior and to create a rhythmic pattern on the exterior walls. Serving multiple functions, the articulated façade diffuses light during the brightest times of the day and transforms the building into a glowing, crystallized beacon during the night.

3XN
Middelfart Savings Bank

Middelfart, Funen, Denmark, 2010

Located by the Lillebælt waters on the island of Funen, this bank serves as both an impressive public space and a striking architectural icon for the town. The building is characterized by a dramatic angled roofscape that accommodates multiple functions. Subtly referencing the maritime environment and the surrounding timber-framed buildings, 83 prism-like skylights compose the surface of the spectacular roof. This articulated roof provides a perfect view toward the water while also shading the interior from direct sunlight. The bank work stations are located on three open terraces internally connected by broad staircases that encourage interaction and informal meetings. All floors enjoy plenty of daylight and unobstructed views of the water.

AART architects
The Culture Yard

Elsinore, Denmark, 2010

Transformed from an old shipbuilding yard, this tessellated glass project consists of a light-filled cultural and knowledge center, concert halls, showrooms, conference rooms, a dockyard museum, and a public library. Designed as a hinge between the past and present, the project reinforces the identity of the local community while expressing an international attitude and architectural curiosity. To reference the area's industrial past, the original concrete skeleton with armored steel has been reinforced but left exposed, while a new layer of faceted glass provides a more contemporary addition to the façade. Fragmented, yet coherent, this triangulated exterior challenges the historic site while reinforcing the relationship between interior and exterior.

right page
Herzog & de Meuron
Museum of Cultures

Basel, Switzerland, 2010

A striking extension to a nineteenth-century structure, this irregularly folded roof resonates with the vernacular of its medieval surroundings. Clad in blackish-green ceramic tiles, the roof refracts light, producing an effect much like that of the finely structured brick tiles on the roofs in the old town. The hexagonal tiles, some of them three-dimensional, are supported by a steel framework that allows for an expressive and column-free gallery underneath. Part of the courtyard has been lowered and an expansive, gently inclined staircase leads down to the museum entrance. Hanging plants and climbing vines lend the courtyard a distinctive atmosphere, and work in concert with the roof to generate a new identity for the museum

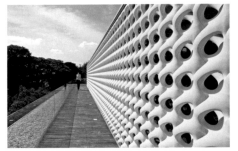

Studio MK27
//Marcio Kogan & Carolina Castroviejo
Cobogó House

São Paulo, Brazil, 2011

This stunning single-family residence applies an ethereal brise-soleil across its exterior. The unusual and highly articulated sunscreen functions as both an organic ornament and a highly efficient diffuser of light. Comprised as a series of high gloss, modular loops, this perforated and softly accentuated façade contrasts with the crisp, rectilinear edges of the house, creating a tactile interplay between the distinctive geometries. At night, the house adopts a shimmering glow, as lights from the interior spaces filter out into the surrounding garden.

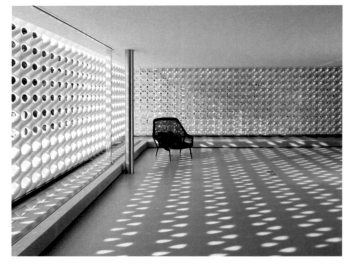

Salto Architects
EMÜ Sports Hall

Tartu, Estonia, 2009

This understated building and its landscaping integrates and organizes the scattered university campus.
Standing prominently along the roadside on the verge
of the city, its location allows the sports hall to serve as
a sort of entry marker for the school. The basic design
idea dictates that one understands this at first glimpse.
The rectangular volume, stretched at each corner, sits
slightly elevated from the ground while entrenching
the main entrance into the landscape. The stretched-
out corners create concave lines both in plan and el-
evation, resulting in unconventional spaces inside and
varying optical effects outside.

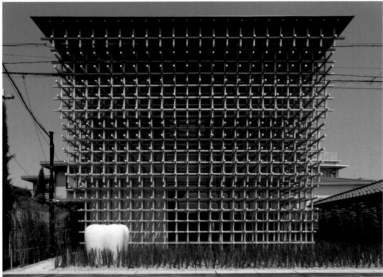

Kengo Kuma & Associates
GC Prostho Museum Research Center

Kasugai-shi, Japan, 2010

Inspired by the logic of a Japanese wooden toy, this gridded project stands as a full-scale embodiment of the traditional system of interlocking elements. Situated in a small mountain town, the entire project comprises a series of wood poles with uniquely shaped joints that can be assembled without a single nail or metal fitting. These repeating members form a cubic grid that becomes a unique, layered structure when applied to the scale of a building. By stacking together a simple, repeating element, this warm and glowing structure showcases the importance and relevance of handcraft, helping to renew its place within the architectural process.

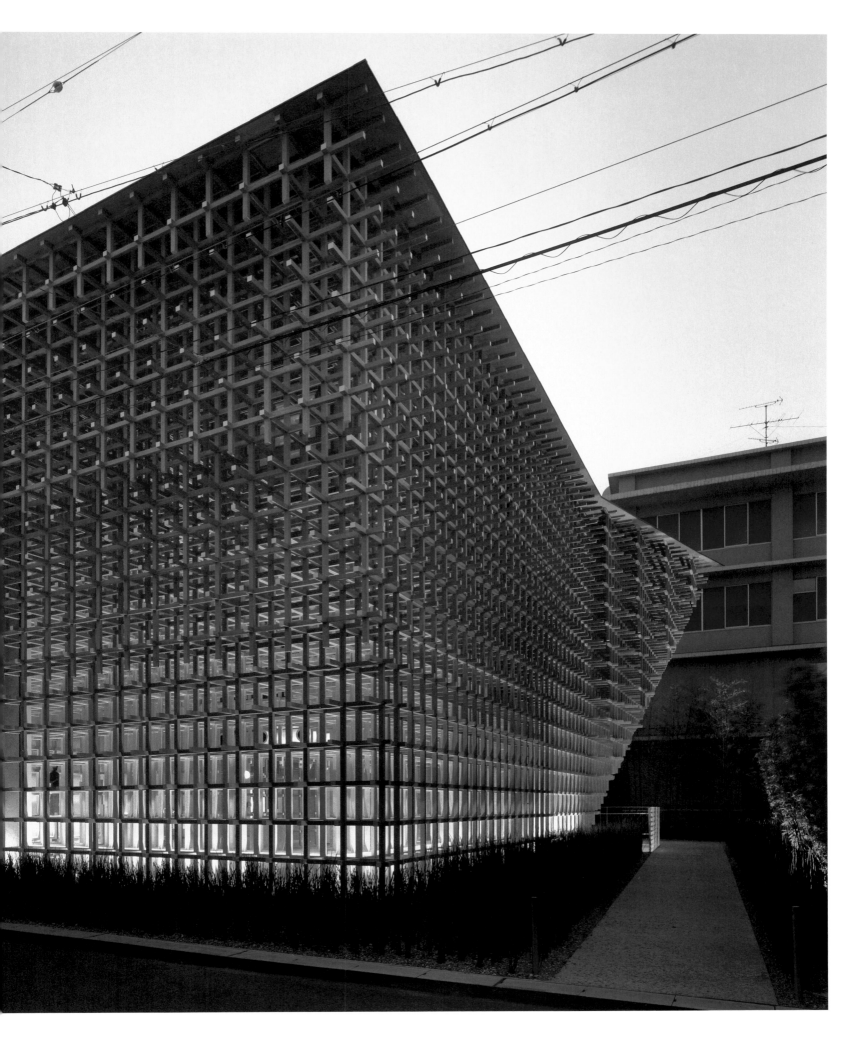

Reiulf Ramstad Architects
Trollwall Restaurant

Trollveggen, Norway, 2011

Located in the Romsdal Valley, this visitor center stands at the base of Europe's tallest vertical, overhanging rock face. The project derives its formal logic from the dramatic mountain ranges surrounding the site. The angular glass façade provides visitors with expansive views to the outdoors while still serving as a protective shelter. These glass surfaces reflect and integrate the pristine natural setting into the appearance of the building, allowing the project and the environment to visually complement one another.

MLRP
Mirror House
Copenhagen, Denmark, 2011

Part of the new Interactive Playground Project in Copenhagen, this project transforms an existing graffiti-plagued playground structure into an inviting and reflective pavilion. Funhouse mirrors are mounted on the gabled ends of the building and behind each door, providing an engaging play experience through the use of distorted perspectives and transformed reflections. Instead of a typical closed façade, the mirrored edges produce a fluid transition between built environment and natural landscape, reflecting the surrounding park and playground activities. At night, the whimsical building hides behind wooden shutters, becoming just another anonymous structure. During the day, the building reopens, attracting children to its mirrors and refracting their images in all directions.

Studio SKLIM
Hansha Reflection House

Nagoya, Japan, 2011

This monolithic residence derives its striking exterior from the programatic needs of the interior. After carving out space for the courtyard, parking of three cars, and a roof deck, the mass is chiseled further to accommodate the structure, daylight, ventilation, and optimal views. With an extensive 3.2 meter wooden cantilever, the house shrugs off the formal expectations of a traditional box dwelling. A centrally-placed window nestles itself into the center of this cantilever, pulling the surrounding surfaces inward while directing views outward.

Cor & Asociados
//Miguel Rodenas &
Jesús Olivares
Music Hall and Auditorium
in Algueña MUCA

Algueña, Spain, 2011

This iridescent box serves as a music hall and cultural space for a small agricultural village. Repurposing and rehabilitating an abandoned building of the civil guard, the understated design intervention clads the structure in shimmering, pearl-colored ceramic panels. To emphasize the subtle yet alluring remodel, the new hall functions as a blind box. By keeping apertures, windows, and doors to an absolute minimum, the surface glitters and refracts in the light without obstruction, creating a recognizable landmark rich in contemporary elegance and historical value.

Takeshi Hosaka
Room Room
Tokyo, Japan, 2010

This playful house functions as an effective communication tool between a deaf couple and their two children. Located in an overcrowded residential area of Tokyo, the interior of this two-story box consists of a series of small rooms organized by the numerous tiny square openings that scatter over the façade, roof, and floors. The cutouts on the floor are used as atriums or practical openings for communication. Engaging one another through sign language, or with the help of props, the family uses these strategic portals to enable an ongoing dialogue between the first and second floors. The wall and roof openings bring air and light into the interior and offer opportunities for communication between the small outdoor garden, rooftop, and interior. Each opening represents a conduit for dialogue, light, and air that extends far beyond its white cubic shell.

109 Architects & Youssef Tohme
USJ Campus de L'Innovation et du Sport

Beirut, Lebanon, 2011

This graphic concrete campus functions as an urban block within the bustling city fabric of Beirut. The main corner of the building lifts up to produce a large sculpted void, providing students with a visual connection to their vibrant urban context and creating a street-level meeting space. The façades of the building are punctuated by a randomized series of apertures that vary in shape, density, and pattern. These openings illuminate the interior with filtered light while establishing a visual identity for the school.

Neri & Hu Design and Research Office
The Waterhouse at South Bund

Shanghai, China, 2010

A new boutique hotel resides within the walls of this existing 1930s headquarters of the Japanese Army. Located in Shanghai's South Bund District, the hotel presents a clear contrast between old and new. The space has undergone a full restoration, with new additions clad in Cor-Ten steel that rise up and over the existing structure, reflecting the site's industrial past. The hotel's rugged concrete interior erases the distinction between inside and outside, public and private, creating a disorienting yet refreshing spatial experience. The public spaces allow one to peek into private rooms, while the private spaces provide glimpses back into the public areas. These visual connections not only add an element of surprise, but also encourage hotel guests to confront the local Shanghai urban condition, where visual corridors and tight adjacencies define the unique spatial flavor of the city.

138

140

Salto Architects
NO99 Straw Theatre

Tallinn, Estonia, 2011

Built on top of one of the best preserved, recently abandoned baroque fortifications of central Tallinn, this temporary theater acknowledges and reactivates its important historical location. A large black rectangular volume serves as the main theater and then cascades down the hillside to form a covered walkway into the building. The dramatic appeal of the project stems from its black, uncompromisingly mute main rectangular hall, which contrasts with the descending, angled corridor. Fabricated from uncovered bales of straw spray-painted black, the theater has a furry, soft texture which is juxtaposed against its refined architectural form.

Ryuji Nakamura
Bang
Tokyo, Japan, 2011

Effectively dividing a nearly empty exhibition space, this ethereal and atmospheric project applies the lightest possible design intervention. A gathering of white ribbons fixed to the ceiling and floor creates a thin curving plane that constantly shifts in transparency depending on where a visitor stands in the space. Oscillating between impenetrable wall and ephemeral ribbon, the project cloaks the fashion exhibition displayed behind it in an immersive fog, adding a sense of mystery and intrigue to the space.

x architekten
Hairstyle Interface
Linz, Austria, 2008

Situated on a quiet Austrian shopping street, this
curving wooden façade renovation provides a striking
new face for an extant hair salon. Creating a three-
dimensional articulated wave from an array of distinctive laminated sheets of wood, the entire façade acts
as an effective advertisement for the store, evoking a
tactile image of flowing hair. The vertical stripes of
waterjet-cut wood bulge toward the top of the façade,
offering an elegant atmosphere while providing privacy for the customers within.

Hertl.Architekten
Aichinger House

Kronstorf, Austria, 2010

A striking 2-story apartment building is the result of a renovation of an existing restaurant with two connected bars. By shrouding the exterior in a light grey curtain, an ordinary building is transformed into something extraordinary. The curtain pulls and pinches to allow geometric glimpses of the building hidden behind and to direct light into the interior. In the evenings, the curtain catches the light from inside, casting a diffused glow over the building. Creating an illusion of a highly articulated and frozen façade, the expressive curtain allows an otherwise unremarkable building to constantly reinvent itself.

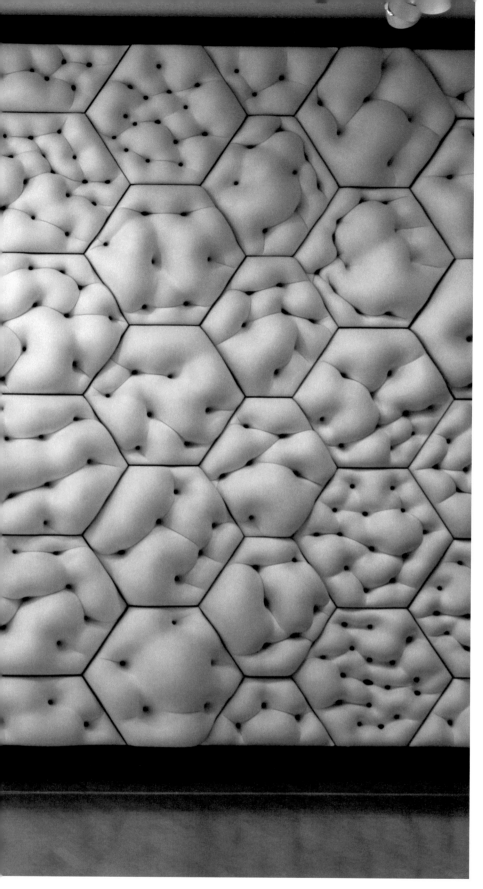

Matsys
//Andrew Kudless
P_Wall

San Francisco, California, USA, 2009

Commissioned for the exhibition Sensate: Bodies and Design at the San Francisco Museum of Modern Art, this organic wall represents part of a series of projects exploring the self-organization of material under force. Using nylon fabric and wooden dowels as form-work, the weight of the liquid plaster slurry causes the fabric to sag, expand, and wrinkle. The result is a series of irregular interlocking hexagonal panels that shift in size and volume. The final effect of these arrayed panels is a voluptuous surface that begs to be touched. Though appearing as an infinitely soft collection of pillows made of marshmallow or meringue, upon closer inspection the rigidity of the articulated surface reveals itself.

rojkind arquitectos & Esrawe Studio
Tori Tori Restaurant

Mexico City, Mexico, 2011

Converted from a residential home, this expressive Japanese restaurant transforms the existing space from the inside out. The interior spaces, articulated by lush panels of vegetation, maintain an intimate and refined feeling while the building's interwoven exterior attracts attention from passersby. The façade, which seems to emerge from the ground, climbs up through the building, mimicking the natural ivy surrounding the retaining walls. Forming an irregular diamond-shaped grid, this eye-catching exterior pattern comprises two self-supporting layers of steel plates which respond to the interior openings, filtering light, shadows, and views throughout the restaurant.

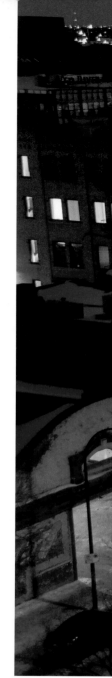

5468796 Architecture
OMS Stage

Winnipeg, Canada, 2010

This psychedelic cube functions as an open-air performance venue set against a backdrop of historic warehouses in Winnipeg's Exchange District. Commissioned following an invited competition, the design creates an alluring stage with year-round relevance for the community. The project consists of a multifunctional environment that shifts from a vibrant performance space to an interactive pavilion as its focal point. Projections displayed on the flexible metal skin transform the cube into an eye-catching beacon for the park, evolving with the seasons and lighting conditions. During performances, the skin of the seemingly regular cube draws back to reveal the concrete structure within and produce a dynamic and inviting exterior surface.

UNStudio
Galleria Centercity
Cheonan, Korea, 2010

Responding to the current retail climate in Asia, where department stores also operate as social and cultural meeting places, this visually saturated project treats the department store as a museum. An expanded interpretation of utility beyond efficiency and profitability lies at the heart of the design, and provides a stimulating experience for the visitor. On the outside, the double-layered façades are articulated in a trompe l'oeil pattern of vertical mullions, resulting in the scale of the building being virtually unreadable. On the inside, this play with scale continues as a layered and varied space that encourages investigation and unfolds as visitors move through the building. Moiré effects, special lighting, and animations, generated by the largest illuminated surface of its kind in the world, ensure that the outside changes appearance constantly. The thematic animated content of this integrated media façade facilitates a more urban approach to branding.

157

Phu Hoang Office &
Rachely Rotem Studio
Exhale Pavilion
Miami Beach, Florida, USA, 2010

This voluminous pavilion for Art Basel Miami Beach functioned as a surreal and interactive outdoor space for public art. Inspired by the shapeless quality of the wind, the project was constructed out of seven miles of reflective and phosphorescent rope. Forming a network of complex catenary curves with built-in swings, the sinuous glimmering pavilion appeared like an expansive chandelier or spider's web. The maximal use of a minimal material resulted in an impressive and expansive canopy for hosting a public forum on the arts.

1024 Architecture
3D-Bridge
Paris, France, 2010

Existing but for a single night, this volumetric project perched atop a bridge in Paris. The sculptural installation used video-mapping, light, and sound augmentation to produce an immersive experience for the senses. The form comprised a series of stacked transparent cubes edged with lighting to attract people from a distance. The giant mass fluctuated in appearance between imposing volume and temporary, translucent structure. Recalling a life-size game of Tetris, the installation engaged an effective mixture of scale, color, and texture to create a lasting impression long after its disassembly.

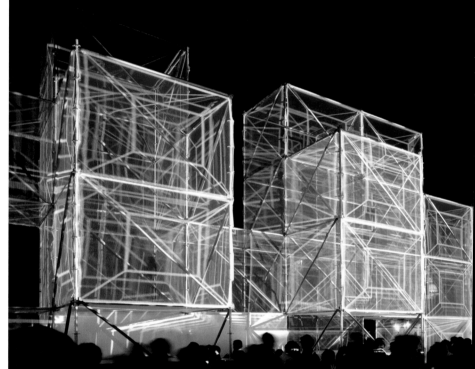

158

b720 Fermín Vázquez Arquitectos
Lleida-Alguaire Airport
Lleida, Spain, 2010

Evoking the subtle glamor of the late 1960s, this softly curved project unifies a terminal building, a control tower, and two storage spaces into a cohesive, sweeping architectural statement. The project ascends as if the landscape were being pulled up to meet the sky, culminating in its highest point, the control tower. Blending into the surrounding scenery while simultaneously becoming a recognizable landmark for the region, the building is blanketed in a large striped envelope of earthy colors, drawing together its various functions and structures. The building lifts up toward the entrances, exposing a wrap-around glass façade that adds to the floating quality of this topographic form.

Aedas Limited
18 Kowloon East

Hong Kong, China, 2010

This eye-catching 28-story mixed-use tower offers an intriguing design synthesis to a rational box on top and a lush garden below. With the building located in a dense industrial section of Kowloon, its design provides a more environmentally sustainable addition to the area, rather than another office tower entirely wrapped in coolly-glazed skin. The building introduces extensive planting on the car park floors at the lower portion of the tower, forming a flowing organic pattern near street level. In addition to the visual greening effect on the neighborhood, the planting also functions as an effective filter, improving general air quality.

24H > architecture
Housing Hatert

Nijmegen, Netherlands, 2011

Part of an extensive renewal effort along the outskirts of the city, this oscillating high-rise represents an iconic landmark for the area. Strips of balconies wind around the perimeter of the building, stretching and bending in numerous directions on the corners, and then retreating to a uniform datum along the sides. These geometric balconies create a dynamic formal composition while providing personalized views from every unit. The irregular balcony bands are additionally wrapped in a perforated metal cladding that allows for subtle patterning to extend across the façade.

Behnisch Architekten //Stefan Behnisch, David Cook & Martin Haas
Marco Polo Tower
Hamburg, Germany, 2010

This shifting tower represents a prominent addition to the port city of Hamburg. The sculptural, 58-unit residential project twists and recoils to offer each apartment a spectacular view of the harbor and surrounding city. Spacious terraces and balconies wrap around the building, extending the living space in a soft play of lines, and giving the tower a distinctive appearance. The recessed façades are shaded by the overhanging curved terraces, eliminating the need for more conventional external shading. Due to the ever-changing external shape of the undulating building, no two floors or apartments are alike.

UNStudio
Education Executive Agency & Tax Offices

Groningen, Netherlands, 2011

Representing a greener approach to high-rise buildings, this 92-meter-tall complex of soft, undulating curves prominently marks the Groningen skyline. The asymmetric, aerodynamic construction sits amidst a small, ancient woodland, sheltering rare and protected wildlife. Housing government agencies that often suffer a reputation of being cold and heartless, the architecture presents these institutions with a softer, approachable, and more human profile. Instead of building yet another harsh and inaccessible tower, this project deliberately cloaks a commanding public institution in an organic, friendlier, and more future-oriented form. A flexible and multidirectional floor plan introduces a new landscape into the building, and bands of ribbon windows extend along the façade, offering sweeping vistas to the outdoors.

Studio Gang Architects
Aqua Tower

Chicago, Illinois, USA, 2010

At 82 stories and over 1.9 million square feet, this flowing tower stands as one of the few high-rises in the world that creates a community through its strategically undulating balconies. With a hotel, apartments, condominiums, parking, offices, and one of Chicago's largest green roofs, this multi-use tower demonstrates both architectural and technical achievements. The project's most distinctive feature, the curving outdoor terraces, differs in shape from floor to floor based on criteria such as views, solar shading, and dwelling type. As these balconies stretch out in one place and then disappear in another, the building achieves a surreal visual quality, appearing as if in constant motion and shifting at a rate nearly impossible for the human eye to resolve. This photorealistic rendering in the sky confounds an understanding of traditional skyscraper aesthetics while creating a strong connection to the outdoors and the city.

169

New York by Gehry at Eight Spruce Street

New York, USA, 2011

The tallest residential tower in both New York City and the Western Hemisphere, this project's distinctively elegant glass and stainless steel silhouette has redefined the Manhattan skyline. The undulating folds in the exterior wall result in an unprecedented variety of residential unit layouts inside and a dynamic and iconic shape outside. The project comprises 903 rental apartments, doctors' offices, and the first-ever public school to be built in New York City on private land.

IBA—Information Based Architecture
//Mark Hemel & Barbara Kuit
Canton TV Tower

Guangzhou, China, 2010

The winning competition entry for redeveloping the center of Guangzhou, this startling tower serves as both a dramatic icon for the city and a marvel of structural engineering. The slender and evocative lattice form proves both simple and complex. Contrasting with the more typical angular, repetitive, and heavy skyscrapers of the past, this tower offers a smooth, curved, and elegant frame that appears to float into the

//x architekten
Pastoral Care Center

//querkraft architekten
TMW Technical Museum Vienna

chapter 04
internal affairs

While the interior of a building serves a number of undeniably pragmatic functions, its more valuable and aesthetically enticing job is to offer sanctuary and respite from the outside world. Wrapping the interior in a protective cloak, architecture's inner realm provides a safe and uplifting haven for thought and introspection. Within these walls awaits a space that promotes a sense of reflection and wonder for its occupants. The interior, more than any other architectural device, offers a form of intimacy that reconnects us with ourselves.

The image of the interior, much like our image of ourselves, evolves constantly. Due to this regular shift in perception, the design of the interior can, and often does, take almost any form. From expansive halls to intimate cave-like nooks, no clear-cut formula exists for developing and staging an emotionally charged and affective internal space.

The interior creates an identity and atmosphere for the occupants of a building. While these inner rooms visually permeate the exterior on occasion, more often than not they remain quite well hidden. Free from the constraints imposed by a building's structure, history, and vernacular, the less connected the interior becomes with its outer shell, the more profound the emotive sensation it produces. The experiential intrigue surrounding this emotional reaction underscores why many sculptural and expressive interiors are so typically associated with demure exteriors.

When moving from the image of the outside to the space on the inside, an aesthetic agenda must still exist. The key difference then lies in understanding that the way this interior design approach is structured and how one eventually occupies it can vary. Whether users of these spaces feel a sense of curiosity, comfort, or confusion relies on the sequence, scale, color, and aesthetic language developed in their designs. Depending on what type of activities, sensations, and identity an architect wants to promote and foster, the look of the interior can change completely from project to project, even when the interior function remains the same.

Unlike the exterior, the interior retains a much closer relationship to scale. Becoming less about conveying a discernible image and more about the development of a suggestive experience or interaction, each interior can function as its own discreet environment and microcosm. Within these spaces, the world can be scaled down to human size, evoking immediate and powerful sensations. On the inside, the world suddenly becomes defined and ordered by the touchable and untouchable, the reachable and unreachable. As almost everything in a room can be touched and engaged with, scale and texture comprise the critical elements for mediating and interpreting the interior.

The interior remains one of the few places where a person can perceive a shift in scale. The transition between inside and outside or between one room and another offers dramatic potential for influencing the emotional reaction generated by its spatial sequence. Architecture's ability to develop recognizable shifts in scale can make us feel small and humble in big spaces and large and protected (or at times claustrophobic) in small spaces.

We experience ourselves through our architecture. Whether we feel huge, tiny, cramped, or endlessly vast, the experience of scale only becomes possible through the presence of contrast. Without the juxtaposition between large and small, low and high, or dark and light, the potency of the interior dulls considerably. With that said, successful interiors offer a bit of everything, enhancing an experience through affective spatial sequencing.

The technique of compression and expansion and the use of reflection serve as two reoccurring spatial tactics that connect these seemingly unrelated projects. Mirrored and glossy surfaces promote a heightened sense of self-awareness, reflecting the self and surrounding spaces within the same interior. This interplay between heavy and light, shiny and matte, creates unexpected visual connections that in turn promote awareness of our role in engaging and activating a space and its sequential logic.

The surprising interpretations of the interior that follow explore a diverse range of aesthetic possibilities for developing emotive and compelling spaces. While these projects encompass temporary and permanent interventions in an array of colors, shapes, and sizes, each example elicits a strong sensorial reaction from its occupants. From Élise Morin and Clémence Eliard's startlingly surreal undulating landscape of discarded CDs to the intimate and ethereal cave-like pavilion of Olga Sanina and Marcelo Dantas, these projects challenge our conventional understanding of the image of an interior and the role it plays in nurturing the human condition.

176

Mathieu Lehanneur
St. Hilaire Church

Melle, France, 2011

Composed of 50 layers of white marble, this project serves as an understated yet visually striking addition to an extant Romanesque church. The serene, undulating topography acts as the main podium for the space and rises and falls based on the programmatic needs of the clergy. The deepest part of the marble landscape dips down to become a pristine sunken pool. The altar and ambo are composed from unusual and massive pieces of patterned stone that both blend with and add definition to their historical surroundings.

179

x architekten
Pastoral Care Center

Linz, Austria, 2011

A stunning secular complex creates an inspiring and visually layered space for worship and reflection. Sunken into the site, the exterior reads as a stealth bunker, guarding the interior within its heavy walls. Upon entering the center, the project opens up to produce an ethereal and highly graphic space washed with light. Thin black stripes that vary in density run along the faceted white walls, accentuating the angle and border of each triangulated surface. Slender lamps embedded into the surface follow the same angles to enhance the geometric interior. The flat yet articulated interior challenges patrons' perceptions of space, creating a sense of awe and visual reverie.

Joey Ho Design
Art House Café

Hangzhou, China, 2010

Situated within a 3-story gallery, this angular and graphic project creates a striking visual identity for the café. Though static, the triangulated space appears in constant motion. Angled surfaces clad in rich wood jump through space and intersect with dramatic white planes of corian and marble. The introduction of a simple triangular repeating element in various dimensions creates a design that defies traditional spatial divisions, enhancing communication between the interior space and its users.

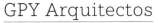

GPY Arquitectos
Tenerife Center of Dramatic Arts

Santa Cruz de Tenerife, Spain, 2003

This dramatic arts center presents itself to the surrounding community as an urban stage, integrating the city and landscape into its backdrop. The interior roofed patio, generated by a three-dimensional folding of the wooden surface, functions as a scenic box that opens toward the city, underscoring its role as a collaborative public forum. Defined as an inclined surface, the patio doubles as an open-air auditorium. This auditorium space also represents the backbone for the pedestrian routes throughout the building, which comprise a system of ramps that connect the different scenic spaces of the center via an oblique zigzag geometry. The entire building can be transformed into a space for performances and public theater. As the audience watches from the ramps, platforms, and landings, it continuously oscillates between spectator and actor.

Suppose Design Office
House in Fukawa

Hiroshima, Japan, 2010

Designed for a family of six, this seemingly normal house offers few exterior clues about its mind-bending interior. Due to heavy traffic in the area, the house remains visually closed on the outside, appearing as an inconspicuous box from the street. An extremely tall and slender door, the only unusual exterior detail of the project, serves as the main entrance to the interior realm. A staircase integrated into the surrounding wooden walls extends from floor to ceiling and stands in the very center of the house. All rooms are connected to this core, resulting in randomly placed spaces with independent levels and angles. The scale and density of the wooden interior distorts any notion of classical perspective. With each room a box, the tops of these spaces can be used for terraces and circulation, adding to the surreal collapsing of one's spatial perception.

Takeshi Hosaka
Daylight House
Yokohama, Japan, 2011

With 29 square skylights installed in the roof, this elegant house, nested in a valley of taller buildings, enjoys natural illumination from the sky. Accommodating a couple with two children, the gridded building begins with a single high-ceilinged space, partitioned to accommodate a bedroom, kids' room, and study. The expansive reach of the diffused light from the curving acrylic ceiling can be felt from any room. By uniformly illuminating the house from the roof, the interior undergoes a rich transformation each day as it absorbs the shifting patterns of light from the sun, moon, and surrounding city.

David Wiseman
Platanus Bibliotechalis
West Hollywood, California, USA, 2011

Located in the grand interior stairwell of the brand new West Hollywood Library, this delicate artwork reflects the relationship between the library and community. Clad in cast porcelain sycamore bark, tree trunks grow from the stairs, sprouting into plastered steel and bronze branches that ascend into the main skylight. Copper, brass, and steel leaves as well as porcelain seed pods emerge from these branches to produce an ethereal yet man-made interpretation of nature. The site-specific installation engages with the large airspace above the stairway, establishing a link between the library and surrounding park. Inspired by the ancient indigenous sycamores of the region, ghostly branches appear through the walls and extend 60 feet into the volume of the space, welcoming people to the library collection as they reach toward the light above.

NUCA Studio
Phill
Bucharest, Romania, 2011

This playful meeting place appeals to the entire family. Accommodating a whimsical playground, multipurpose room, small café, and gourmet restaurant, each space utilizes bright white walls accented with colorful highlights and rounded edges, inspired by the designers' love of comic books and animation. The playground and multipurpose room are enclosed areas with independent light and acoustic scenarios, accommodating activities from theater and puppet shows to martial arts and ballet lessons. Upstairs, the dining area retains an open layout with a direct link to the lobby. To add to the surreal quality of the project, a giant white cartoon elephant hovers in the central stairway and peaks into each floor, creating a humorous visual connection between the different levels and functions.

Tjep.
//Frank Tjepkema, Leonie Janssen & Jeroen van Laarhoven
Fabbrica Bergen

Bergen, Netherlands, 2011

This unique restaurant offers an array of elevated seating modules that create a personal and memorable dining experience. These wooden dining pods rely on an authenticity of material, exposing and enhancing the raw nature of the wood grain with softly filleted edges. The interior of each module is stained in soft shades of brown and green, adding a graphic quality to the walls. The more conventional seating area near the wood-fueled kitchen enjoys a wall filled floor to ceiling with logs for the oven, adding a rustic texture and scent to the modern space.

Mathieu Lehanneur
JWT Headquarters

Neuilly-sur-Seine, France, 2011

Evoking the lair of a classic James Bond villain, this advertising agency's headquarters provide a highly tactile and unusual work space. The main meeting and conference rooms are made out of recycled paper pulp, creating massive and organic focal points for the office that add to the project's pronounced visual identity. Clusters of white blocks offer informal seating areas and a green pathway winds its way through the space, producing a sense of directionality and graphic quality. Plants hanging from the ceiling at the entry play music when they come in contact with humans and their musical selection is curated entirely by the members of the agency.

ODBC
//Odile Decq
Phantom—Restaurant of the Garnier Opera

Paris, France, 2011

Like a phantom, silent and insidious, the soft curves of this mezzanine-level restaurant hover above the dinner guests, covering the space with a surface that bends and undulates. Located behind the columns of the east facade of the Opera Garnier, the restaurant follows strict guidelines concerning the historical character of the monument, while still creating a striking and immersive interplay between old and new. Without being allowed to touch any wall, pillar, or ceiling, the façade of the restaurant comprises a veil of undulating glass, sliding between each column. With all structure smartly hidden, the glass provides clear views with minimal impact to the building. The sensuous red and white interior functions as a continuous surface, floating between the existing elements of the room without touching them, affirming the project's historically integrated yet undeniably contemporary character.

Ramón Esteve
Myrtus Convention Center

Valencia, Spain, 2009

This ephemeral convention center offers a continuity between spaces achieved by its organic, circular geometry. The building's sinuous shell line grants the space with an understated elegance. Following this undulating line, a series of alternating planes of glass and white concrete create a rhythmic, fluid pattern along the exterior. These intermittent openings offer a visual connection between the gardens and the interior, blurring the boundary between inside and outside. A network of hovering, white circular pieces of varying diameters form a permeable drop ceiling, exposing the building's structure between its gaps.

querkraft architekten
//Jakob Dunkl, Gerd Erhartt &
Peter Sapp
TMW Technical Museum Vienna

Vienna, Austria, 2010

This project resides in the foyer of the historical technical museum's minimalist steel glass extension from the 1990s. Fraught with major fluctuations in temperature, poor acoustics and ventilation, and less than ideal visitor circulation, this project dramatically improves upon the troubled extant foyer space. The primary design intervention for the space incorporates an array of multifunctional and richly expressive furniture pieces made of glass-fiber reinforced plastic and fabric. This eye-catching furniture provides seating, shade, and acoustic absorption, and by night fills the room with white and blue glowing light. These objects, which resemble both abstracted trees and Frank Lloyd Wright's Johnson Wax building, formally envelope the steel columns in the space and offer a visual mediation between the old and new areas of the museum.

Situ Studio
reOrder: An Architectural Environment

Brooklyn, New York, USA, 2011

Responding to the ongoing architectural evolution of the Brooklyn Museum, this project explores the ideals of proportion and ornament that figure so centrally into the design of the building's Great Hall. Augmented by a new set of ordering principles that challenge the colossal scale and regularity of the gridded space, the installation uses a lightweight and flexible fabric construction to exaggerate and reinterpret the traditional colonnade. Integrating strategies developed in the textile industry for folding and gathering, the resulting forms create a system of flexible, tilted, and glowing canopies with built-in benches and tables. These luminescent multipurpose mushrooms offer a new logic to the museum's architectural order, creating a unique forum for public interaction and assembly.

Ronan & Erwan Bouroullec
Textile Field

London, United Kingdom, 2011

Conceived as an expansive, striated interior landscape, this project attempts to humanize and personalize the often intimidating and cold atmosphere of a museum. The gently inclining surface is built from colored foam and textile pieces that produce a sensual field for lounging and enjoying the surrounding artwork and space. The temporary installation offers an inviting carpet of blues, greens, and grays for contemplating the cultural and spatial context in a new and more comfortable way.

Mathieu Lehanneur
Studio 13/16, Centre Pompidou

Paris, France, 2010

This whimsical space functions as a permanent lounge and recreation area for teenage visitors of the Centre Pompidou. The project features a twisting, multipurpose lighting track that can be used for both filming and installations and adds a dynamic compositional element to the space. A playful, light blue topography with built-in DVD players, televisions, and music systems fills the perimeter of the room and doubles as a platform for seating and relaxation. Conceived as a hybrid television, cinema, and music studio, this project offers teenagers a dramatic space for action and creation.

Kimihiko Okada
Another Geography

Tokyo, Japan, 2008

This vast inverted landscape grows out of a Diesel clothing store's ceiling, transforming the space into a glittering cave full of stalactites. Appearing as an utterly massive geological finding, the actual form is comprised solely of crumpled aluminum foil. Shaped by one of the thinnest, lightest, and most flexible metals, yet maintaining an appearance of extreme density and volume, the installation beckons visitors into the precariously confounding space. Fluctuating between imposing mass and floating surface, this project evokes the classic principles of the sublime with its provocative and foreboding illusions of scale and weight.

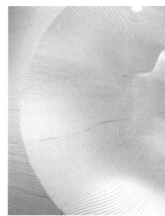

this page

Vazio S/A
//Carlos Teixeira
The Same, the Other

São Paulo, Brazil, 2010

Part of the São Paulo Art Biennial 2010, this geometric project served as a dynamic arena for dance, theater, and music. Created out of densely stacked layers of cardboard, the installation comprised an array of angled and curved pieces which allowed for a variety of formal arrangements. The project departed from a traditional closed shape, becoming an engaging labyrinth that could shrink and expand as needed. Becoming wall, floor, partition, and even furniture, this complex network of cardboard produced a highly tactile experience for engaging and structuring space.

right page

Ryumei Fujiki
Artificial Topography

Kobe, Japan, 2011

Composed of 1,000 layered sheets of soft plastic, this contoured white void provides a tactile, cylindrical space for resting and exploring. Built-in lights illuminate the different layers of the undulating interior, emphasizing the distinctive yet unified elements. The amorphous and cave-like space doubles as both an artwork and a giant monochromatic furniture piece. With every surface soft and pliable, visitors can explore the rippled interior to find a space suited for their unique body types.

Olga Sanina & Marcelo Dantas
The House of Books

Madrid, Spain, 2008

This temporary layered pavilion served as part of the Madrid Book Fair. Inspired by the book as a design object, the surreal project derived its inspiration from the volume, mass, and multiple pages of a book. The ethereal interior of the space gave visitors the sensation of slipping between and carving through the undulating white pages of a giant novel. The project's curving layers created cave-like passageways that beckoned from the exterior and offered a tactile, light-filled gathering space on the interior.

52 students from the Faculty of Interior Design, Academy of Fine Arts, Munich
The Third Room

Munich, Germany, 2008

This surreal organic topography is the result of the efforts of 52 art students using 1,292,300 recyclable zip ties. The walkable installation extends across a 200-square-meter space, transforming the Munich Modern Art Museum into a glowing, white, anamorphic wonderland. Bulging from both the ground and the ceiling, the two surfaces rise up and dip down to connect with each other, appearing as a series of stalagmite and stalactite formations. The countless zip ties produce a fur-like texture across the space, creating the illusion that one is traversing an infinitely soft ice cave.

214

Tomás Saraceno
Biosphere

Statens Museum for Kunst, Copenhagen, Denmark, 2009

Part ecological bounce house and part gravity-defying mind-bender, this anamorphic project fills a corridor connecting the old and new buildings of a Danish art museum. These hovering biospheres made of plastics and wrapped with tensile cables vary in size and function. Several of the spheres house unusual plant-based ecosystems, while others are filled with water. Visitors can step inside the biggest of the transparent globes that hangs 10 meters above the glistening marble floor, provoking a fascinating yet unsettling feeling of precarious safety. By augmenting one's innate preconceptions of reality, this installation invites alternative methods for experiencing and interacting with one's surroundings and each other.

Élise Morin &
Clémence Eliard
Waste Landscape

Paris, France, 2011

This glistening installation consists of 500 square meters of artificial undulating landscape clad in an armor of 65,000 unsold or repurposed CDs. The surreal topography reminds visitors of the tremendous waste associated with CDs after they gradually disappear from our daily lives. Made of petroleum, the shining slick of CDs forms a still sea of metallic dunes, which reflects images of the surrounding buildings and people passing through. The artwork's monumental scale abstracts an otherwise mundane object, transforming it into an awe-inspiring refracting landscape.

Mihály Balázs Architects //Mihály Balázs, Tamás Tarnóczky & Balázs Tatár

Regional Library and Knowledge Center

Pécs, Hungary, 2010

This unusual library revolves around a dramatic central stairwell that extends through the center of its six levels. From the inside of the library, the stairwell appears to be a monolithic white cone, with a scattering of rectangular windows providing the only ornament. Sheltered within this tapered form hides the impressive main stair. The rounded walls are covered in a floor to ceiling mosaic that accentuates the organic nature of the space. Composed from bands of triangular tiles, the mosaic creates large ribbons of color that evoke the realms of both heaven and earth. The rich blue of the ceiling is flecked with yellow and red highlights, elegantly mimicking the night sky and producing an inspiring transition into the world of learning.

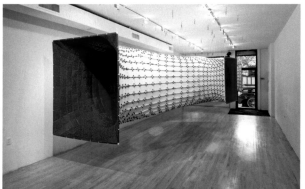

SOFTlab
CHROMAtex.me

New York, USA, 2011

This site-specific installation creates a complex environmental and spatial combination from 4,000 laser-cut panels of photo inkjet paper. Each panel retains a unique shape and custom color. These colors mix inside the form, resulting in a vibrant, shining interior and a more practical white exterior. The panels are connected using a structural network of over 17,000 binder clips and reinforced with a series of acrylic rings. The overall form, integrated with a series of viewing portals, is hung from the ceiling of the gallery, with the largest portal attached to the street-facing window to draw people into the space. Viewers are invited to look into the rich-colored interior only to enter the gallery and find an all-white exterior textured in binder clips.

SOFTlab
(n)arcissus

Frankfurt, Germany, 2010

Suspended in the center of the stairwell at the Frankfurt Kunstverein, this dazzling installation stands nine meters tall. Two large metal rings, one at the top of the stairwell and one attached to the lobby ceiling, support the shimmering structure. The form, comprised of 1,000 custom panels of mylar, changes from a square to an x shape based on the position of the panels in relation to the space. Two of these layers shift in reverse to produce a gradated color on the outside. Functioning as both object and spatial intervention, the reflective project connects the three floors of the building through a translucent and tactile form.

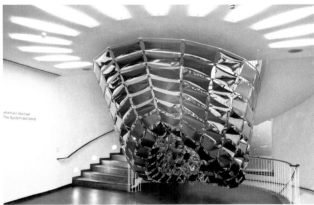

Serge Salat
Beyond Infinity II

Jinan, Suzhou, Shanghai, Beijing, Chengdu, Dalian, Xi'An, Shenzhen, Wuhan, and Changsha, China, 2011

Blending Eastern Chinese philosophy and cosmic visions with advanced contemporary techniques, this traveling installation presents a full-scale private cosmos for visitors. The combination of electronic art, music, sculpture, and architecture results in an immersive labyrinth of mirrors and light. Appearing as an infinite cubic room, three-dimensional timber grids sprinkled over the reflective walls and ceiling take on expansive and confounding shapes as they blur into their own reflections. This endless sea of color and volume develops tantalizing forms only possible in the world of smoke and mirrors.

//Reiulf Ramstad Architects
Trollstigen National Tourist Route Project

//J. MAYER H. Architects
New Airport Building

chapter 05
point of view

//Giancarlo Mazzanti
Spain Library

//Foster + Partners
Spaceport America

//RO & AD Architecten
Moses Bridge

//Peter Zumthor & Louise Bourgeois
Steilneset: Witch Trial Memorial

Architecture has much to learn from nature. While the primary function of architecture is to keep nature out by providing a shelter that protects from predators and extreme shifts in climate, the value of the wild and organic in informing design choices and improving the psychological impact of our buildings is regularly overlooked. By engaging with the outdoors instead of simply turning one's back to it, a new wealth of architectural possibilities arises.

Forms that embrace the natural environment as an integral part of their design agenda represent an inspiring addition to the sculptural architecture movement. Unwrapping the enclosure to instigate a more fluid relationship between indoors and outdoors results in a dramatic vernacular language. This refreshing style generates projects that visually and spatially frame their own unique slice of nature. Through the strategic use of apertures, integrated gardens, terraces, walkways, and lookouts, the architectural intervention and its surroundings engage in a spectacular dialogue that complements and enhances the aesthetic impact of each.

Such a simple yet effective architectural approach takes the concept of the building and transforms it into a strategic framing device for viewing the great outdoors. The technique of choreographing views instills within us a feeling that this endless nature does in fact have a scale, logic, and order. Developing a sense of space and intimacy in a wild setting quiets our feelings of vulnerability by giving us something to which we can both hold on and relate. These feelings are most effectively translated into architectural expression through bold, geometric gestures that cantilever over the edge of steep cliffs or embed themselves deep into the earth.

Although people are drawn to the wild and dangerous, the vast majority prefer the sensation of impending trouble more than its actual manifestation, which is where architecture comes in. There are few things more exhilarating than staring down at the hazards of the outside world from a safe interior which dissolves just one step ahead. The existence of the line (no matter how fine) between danger and safety lies at the heart of the most sublime architectural expressions, many of which engage this sensation through the inherent visual drama present in nature.

Projects that successfully blur the boundary between inside and outside maintain an effective combination of both shelter and vantage point. The visceral impact established by the framing of nature as opposed to merely the framing of another familiar urban environment depends on the extreme juxtaposition between the natural and the man-made to maintain its power. By providing just the right amount of exposure and security, people are able to engage with their natural environment in a much more profound way. Through their sheltering qualities, these sites of pilgrimage establish an even stronger sense of visibility and connection to the wilderness.

The oscillation between inside and outside remains visually and emotionally exhilarating due to our innate sense of imagination. Occupying the inside half of a structure that straddles the natural inevitably makes us think more about the half left outside. Such an experience can be achieved by conceiving a project from outside to inside or conversely from inside to outside. HHF architects' Ruta del Peregrino and Ryue Nishizawa's Teshima Museum serve as two provocative examples of the technique of beginning with the outdoors and working inward. Both of these impressive concrete forms approach nature as an untouched canvas, gradually framing key parts of the outdoor space to form the interior. The alternative approach, exemplified by Christian Pottgiesser's Maison L and Peter Zumthor and Louise Bourgeois's Steilneset Memorial, starts by developing an interior condition and then systematically breaking it apart to create connections to the outside. Both models, diametrically opposed in technique, cultivate spaces that leverage from their exterior surroundings in order to define their interiors.

The act of engaging with nature strips away one's preconceptions, promoting a purer form of perception. The architecture that follows reconnects both the building and its occupants to the environment. Extending past the typical aesthetic stereotypes which separate indoor and outdoor living and merely add some windows here and some plants there to connect them, these stunning projects serve as a collective and undeniably appealing call for a return to the wild.

Takeshi Hosaka
Hoto Fudo

Yamanashi, Japan, 2009

Set at the base of Mt. Fuji, this organic building becomes a natural visual extension of the surrounding mountains and clouds. The soft, almost fluffy geometry remains open to the air during most seasons. A series of interior vaults elegantly accentuates the undulating surface. These silky arches accommodate an expansive, interconnected dining space that winds across the entire building. Referencing the arched language of the interior, large semicircles that are cut into the mass serve as both the main entrances and the only apertures in the building. This ethereal and evocative rippled mass, though made from the strongest of concretes, gives a sensation of dining in the lightest of clouds.

Dellekamp Arquitectos //with Rozana Montiel/ Periférica
Void Temple—Ruta del Peregrino

Cerro del Obispo, Mexico, 2010

Part of the Ruta del Peregrino pilgrimage, this hovering concrete circle uses its formal language to channel the universal symbol of unity, a meaning that transcends cultures, borders, and languages. Appearing time and again within religious rituals and depictions, the use of the circle in this project represents the cyclical, never-ending journey of the traveling pilgrims. The pristine ring offers a monumental and inspiring place of reflection for the pilgrims to look back upon their journey before continuing on toward their final destination.

Dellekamp Arquitectos //with Tatiana Bilbao
Gratitude Open Chapel— Ruta del Peregrino

Lagunillas, Mexico, 2011

Four white concrete slabs welcome pilgrims to the beginning of the route leading to the sanctuary of the Virgin of Talpa. Framed against the sky, these white monoliths angle toward one another, creating the sensation of occupying a tranquil outdoor room. These timeless forms act as a type of protective sentinel and temple of light. Drawing pilgrims toward its sublime form, the affective project offers a serene space for silence, peace, and self-reflection.

HHF architects
Lookout Point—Ruta del Peregrino

Jalisco, Mexico, 2011

Yet another striking concrete addition along the Ruta del
Peregrino, this spiraling form establishes an iconic nar-
rative with the extraordinary landscape. Functioning
as an additional loop in the pilgrim's path, the round
shape formally anticipates one's movement around the
platform while ascending to admire the surrounding
countryside. The asymmetric arched openings connect
to an open hall covered by a rooftop viewing platform.
The four tangential inner walls are a shifted repetition
of the primary façade. Two staircases located between
these inner circles define a route up to the platform
and back down. A brick wall with a cross-shaped opening represents the only exception to the curved logic
of the project. This straight surface becomes the most
protected part of the building, serving as an intimate
room for resting and prayer.

Office of Ryue Nishizawa
Teshima Art Museum

Teshima Island, Japan, 2010

Embedded in the forest along the Teshima Island waterfront, this ephemeral, white museum resembles an opaque droplet of water frozen in the midst of gliding across the land. Two massive oculi penetrate the softly curved shape, bringing light, air, sound, and water into the space to physically and visually connect the project with its natural surroundings. Created from a 25-cm-thick concrete shell, the project enjoys a space devoid of any pillars or visible structural interference. Unlike standard museums that close off the interior from the exterior with panes of glass, walls, or windows, this project remains completely open to the elements, which allows for an ongoing negotiation between the man-made and the natural.

Shingo Masuda, Katsuhisa Otsubo & Yuta Shimada
Little Hilltop with Wind View

Yamaguchi, Japan, 2010

This project stands as the result of a request from a wind power company to build a tower with a view to the windmill on the property. The unadorned white tower has a minimal number of apertures cut from its façade that not only highlight the windmill but also frame views of the landscape and sky. A simple chair with exaggerated legs sits inside this slender building, providing an elevated platform for enhanced viewing. Inspired by the subtle swaying of the windmill and the surrounding grass, flowers, and clouds, the striking white monolith is engineered with a bent steel structure, allowing it to shift slightly in the wind. This minimal manipulation produces a slight sway and gives a unique slant to the natural scenery.

architecturespossibles
//Christian Pottgiesser
Maison L

Paris, France, 2011

This remarkable home and orangery lies in a pristine forest clearing less than a half hour drive from the center of Paris. Adding on to the extant orangery building from the eighteenth century, the renovation places five 3-story towers into the complex. These striking, minimalist white volumes contrast with the heavy stone of the older building, creating a dynamic exchange between past and present. Glazings around each tower provide natural lighting and offer an intriguing succession of perspectives around and between the property, as well as an overview of the Parisian skyline.

SeARCH & CMA
Villa Vals

Vals, Switzerland, 2009

Scooped out of an alpine mountain slope, this sunken holiday home keeps the pristine natural surroundings unobstructed by burying the entirety of its architecture underground. The intriguing house consists of a slanted façade set into an inclined central patio, with an array of window openings cut from it. Organized around this main façade, the interior features a compact layout of bedrooms with bunk beds, elevated bathrooms, and raised podiums with king-size beds. To keep the site as untouched as possible, the only entrance to the house is through an underground tunnel accessed via a nearby old barn. The steep, angled circular patio offers a stunning frame for viewing nature and connecting with the outdoors from any part of the house.

24H > architecture
Panyaden School

Chiang Mai, Thailand, 2011

Situated in the lush green surroundings of a former
fruit orchard, this expressive 5,000-square-meter bilin-
gual primary school consists of an informal arrangement of thatched pavilions organized along winding
pathways. Load-bearing walls made from rammed
earth form the partitions for the classrooms, while the
outer walls are constructed from adobe. A combination
of glass windows, framed by recycled local hardwood,
bottles, and washing machine windows, all bring natural light into the classrooms. Cupboards, shelves, and
secret play areas are built into the surrounding adobe
walls. The curved contours of the bamboo roof evoke
the impressive formations of the mountains surrounding the site. A larger pavilion, supported by bamboo-
bundled columns, functions as the assembly hall and
canteen and evokes a feeling of walking through a
dense bamboo forest.

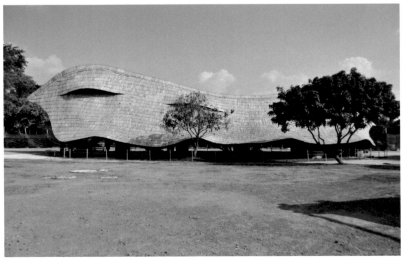

Peter Zumthor & Louise Bourgeois
Steilneset: Witch Trial Memorial

Vardø, Norway, 2011

This striking yet somber collaboration between architect and artist serves as the new memorial to commemorate the victims burned in the seventeenth-century witch hunts. Located adjacent to the assumed execution site, two autonomous forms, one indoor and one outdoor, communicate the severity of these historical events. The compact outdoor pavilion installation stands as the final completed work of artist Louise Bourgeois and comprises a chair from which gas flames emerge and are reflected in seven encircling oval mirrors. Peter Zumthor's slender and rounded building sits adjacent to the outdoor cube. This 125-meter-long exhibition hall erected on wooden piles has 93 illuminated windows, one for each victim burned at the stake in Vardø.

//Peter Zumthor & Louise Bourgeois
Steilneset: Witch Trial Memorial

Salto Architects
Exhibition Grounds of the Estonian Road Museum

Varbuse, Estonia, 2010

The open-air exhibition grounds of this surreal museum are based upon a winding road carved into the earth. A figure-8 shaped path cuts through the site where functions with different characters and scales are placed in succession like a comic strip. A variety of landscapes greet visitors, establishing a compelling dialogue between artificial and natural environments. The sunken outdoor route ranges from 10 centimeters to 4 meters in depth, forming more than 13,000 square meters of visually confounding exhibition space. All but invisible except from aerial view, the dramatic changes in height of this outdoor space blur understandings of scale, depth, and sense of place. The structure is built of reinforced concrete, with authentic historical objects, including a roadside pub, a gas station, a bridge, and a segment of railroad, adding graphic content and a dream-like quality to the project.

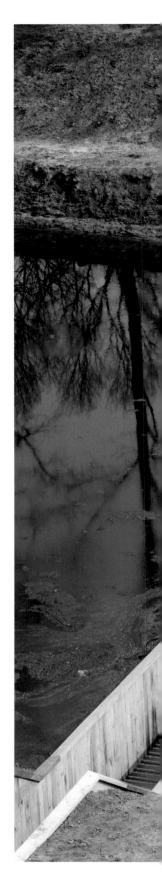

RO&AD Architecten
Moses Bridge

Halsteren, Netherlands, 2011

This biblically inspired sunken bridge provides access across a seventeenth-century moat to the large Fort de Roovere. Constructed out of waterproof wood, this almost invisible bridge lies like a trench between the fortress and the moat, blending in with the outlines of the landscape. As the waterline and ground extend all the way up to its edge, the bridge cannot be seen from a distance, maintaining the illusion of the impenetrable fortress. When viewed up close, the waters appear to part, creating a sublime pathway that can vanish at any moment with a change of the tide.

Luca Gentilcore & Stefano Testa
LEAP: Living Ecological Alpine Pod

Courmayeur, Italy—Mont Blanc, 2011

This modular alpine refuge for mountaineers and climbers creates a minimal impact on the environment while achieving a design rich in dramatic effect. Located on a massive glacier, half of the project cantilevers precariously off the side of a steep cliff. The red and white exterior patterning, filleted edges, and portal windows all add to the surreal and timeless quality of the module. Hovering on a ledge between past and future, this cutting-edge yet infinitely retro pod combines state of the art technology with a bold sense of gravity-defying wonder.

Jarmund/Vigsnæs AS Architects MNAL
Dune House

Suffolk, England, 2010

Situated along the Suffolk coastline, this unusual house replaces an existing building at the site. The dramatic angles of the roofscape prove both strikingly modern and deeply connected to the surrounding traditional building vernacular of the British seaside. The ground floor stands in stark contrast to the upper level both in terms of design and transparency. The glass living area and the terraces on the lower level nestle into the dunes in order to protect against strong winds, while remaining open in all other directions to allow for wide views. The corners can be opened by sliding doors that emphasize the surreal floating appearance of the top floor.

Steven Holl Architects &
Solange Fabião
Cité de l'Océan et du Surf
Museum

Biarritz, France, 2011

A serene set of glowing boxes tucked into a massive
sunken plaza lined with cobblestones comprise the
setting for this museum of ocean ecology and environmental awareness. The building derives its spatial
concept from the surrounding sky and sea. The sky
influences the concave shape of the central gathering
plaza, while the sea finds its formal logic within the
convex structural ceiling forms of the main exhibition
spaces. This concept generates a unique profile and
form for the building while simultaneously referencing its connection to nature. Through its careful inser-
tion and efficient site utilization, this evocative project
integrates seamlessly into the surrounding landscape.

J. MAYER H. Architects
New Airport Building

Mestia, Georgia, 2010

Situated in a medieval UNESCO World Heritage Site and famous ski-resort region, this torqued black and white building provides an eye-catching entry point to the area. The airport is comprised of three distinct and irregular geometries, two of which reach up toward the sky and surrounding mountains. While the exterior is clad in a tinted black glazing with thick white trim, the interior exposes the project's complex structure, providing an irregular and shifting frame for viewing the dramatic landscape.

Estudio Barozzi Veiga
//Fabrizio Barozzi, Alberto Veiga
Headquarters of the Regulatory Board of the Denomination of Origin Ribera del Duero

Roa, Spain, 2011

This unassuming project serves as a transitional element between city and landscape. While clad in traditional stone from the region, the angular tower transforms the local architectural vernacular into something contemporary. The timeless monolith suspended over the plateau reveals few clues about the modern, white interior hidden inside. Standing in stark contrast to the earth-toned, rugged surroundings, the interior of this office boasts clean lines and a playful series of circular windows that flood the space with sunlight.

Giancarlo Mazzanti
Spain Library
Medellin, Colombia, 2007

Perched atop one of the hillsides of Medellin most affected by the violence caused by the drug trafficking of the 1980s, this iconic library stands as the realized effort of the Mayor to provide equal opportunities in social and economic development to the local community. Responding to the hidden and irregular contours of the surrounding mountains, the building organizes its spatial layout around the aesthetic of the folded and clipped planes present within its natural surroundings. This library becomes both a building, a beacon, and a landscape, blending in and reframing its scenic context. Small openings are cut from the exterior, creating a warm interior atmosphere that transports users away from their immediate poverty and into a safe space for reflection and study.

259

Foster + Partners
Spaceport America
Las Cruces, New Mexico, USA, 2011

This unusual desert structure stands as the world's first space terminal for tourists. Dug into and emerging from the surrounding mesa, the low-rise building is entered through a cleft between its two massive wings. These oversized wings evoke a sense of flight while still emphasizing a strong connection to the earth and the building's remote context. Full-height glazing wraps around the back end of the building, which faces onto the runway, providing unobstructed views of takeoffs and landings.

Index

HHF architects
Switzerland | www.hhf.ch
Lookout Point—Ruta del Peregrino
Team: Tilo Herlach, Simon Hartmann, Simon Frommenwiler, Alexa den Hartog, Janna Jessen
Photography by Iwan Baan (upper image), Sergio Pirrone (bottom image)
page 230

IBA—Information Based Architecture
Mark Hemel & Barbara Kuit
Netherlands | www.iba-bv.com
Canton TV Tower
Competition Design Team: Mark Hemel, Barbara Kuit, Taco Hylkema, Patty lui, Nate Kolbe, Stefan Al, Roumpini Makridou, Eva Prelovsek, Daniel Schiffelers | Design Team: Tim Den Dekker, Rena Logara, Xiao Lan Lin, Kuo Jze Yi, Ying He, Danny Marks, Moe Ekabop, Anna Schepper | Structure: Arup
Photography by Information Based Architecture
pages 172–173

Ikimono Architects
Takashi Fujino
Japan | www.sites.google.com/site/ikimonokenchiku
Static Quarry
Ikimono Architects, Charge: Takashi Fujino, Tatsuya Morita, Takahiro Machida | Planning: Satoshi Ida/TTA Inc | Structural engineer: Emiko Sukegawa/ Structural Design firm Accurate, Charge/ Eiko Sukegawa | Landscape: Atsuo Ota/ ACID NATURE 0220, Charge/Atsuo Ohta, Tetsuo Matsushima | General constructors: HASHIZUME Industrial Inc., Charge/Kunio Kobayashi, Kiyoshi Karasawa, Yutaka Aoki | Air, sanitary: Tokue-Setsubi, Charge/Hiroshi Tokue | Electricity: Johoku-Denkikoji, Charge/Toshiyuki Koizumi
Photography by Takashi Fujino/ Ikimono Architects
pages 84–85

J. MAYER H. Architects
Germany | www.jmayerh.de
Metropol Parasol
Project Architect: Jürgen Mayer H., Andre Santer, Marta Ramírez Iglesias | Project Team: Ana Alonso de la Varga, Jan-Christoph Stockebrand, Marcus Blum, Paul Angelier, Hans Schneider, Thorsten Blatter, Wilko Hoffmann, Claudia Marcinowski, Sebastian Finck
Photography by David Franck
pages 8–11
—
Sarpi Border Checkpoint
Project Team: Juergen Mayer H., Jesko Malkolm Johnsson-Zahn, Christoph Emenlauer | Architects on Site: Beka Pkhakadze, Ucha Tsotseria | Building Company: JSC Transmsheni | Structural Engineering: LTD BWC | Structural Engineering of Tower: Nodar Edisherashvili | HVAC: LTD Ecocomfort
Photography by Jesko Malkolm Johnsson-Zahn (page 52/upper left and upper right image, page 53) and

Beka Pkhakadze (page 52/bottom left and bottom right image)
pages 52–53
New Airport Building
Project Team: Juergen Mayer H., Jesko Malkolm Johnsson-Zahn, Hugo Reis, Mehrdad Mashaie, Max Reinhardt
Photography by J. Mayer H.
pages 254–255

Jarmund/Vigsnæs AS Architects MNAL
Norway | www.jva.no
Dune House
Architects: Einar Jarmund, Håkon Vigsnæs, Alessandra Kosberg & Anders Granli | Collaborating architect: Mole Architects Ltd.
Photography by Nils Petter Dale
pages 250–251

Joey Ho Design Ltd
Hong Kong, China | www.joeyhodesign.com
Art House Café
Joey Ho | Other Designer: Yuki Leung, Momoko Lai
Photography by Mr. Wu Yong Chang
pages 182–183

Kengo Kuma & Associates
Japan | www.kkaa.co.jp
GC Prostho Museum Research Center
Cooperation for Design: Design Department of Matsui Construction | Structural Design: Jun Sato Structural Design | Utilities, Equipment: P.T. Morimura & Associates, Ltd | Construction: Matsui Construction | Lighting: Daiko Electrics | Signage: Nippon Design Center Inc, Hara Design Institute
Photography by Daici Ano
pages 120–121

Kimihiko Okada
Japan | www.ookd.jp
Another Geography
Photography by Mikio Shuto
pages 206–207

Luca Gentilcore & Stefano Testa
Italy | www.gandolfigentilcore.com | www.cliostraat.com | www.leapfactory.it
LEAP: Living Ecological Alpine Pod
Architects: Luca Gentilcore/Gandolfi & Gentilcore, Stefano Testa/Cliostraat; Design Team: Edoardo Boero, Marilena Cambuli, Massimo Teghille | Structural engineering: Luca Olivari/ Olivari Composite Engineering: Andrea Bruzzone | Electrical engineering: EDF-ENR spa, Carlo Sasso, Andrea Sasso, Giampaolo Pittatore, Enrico Pons | Other consultants: Alberto Morino (geologia) Federico Valfrè di Bonzo (nivologia e valanghe) | Brand Design: Undesign, Massimo Teghille
Photography by Francesco Mattuzzi
page 246

Lyons
Australia | www.lyonsarch.com.au
John Curtin School of Medical Research Stage 1, The Australian National University
Photography by John Gollings Photography
pages 56–57

MAD
China | www.i-mad.com
Ordos City Museum
Directors: Ma Yansong, Yosuke Hayano, Dang Qun | Design Team: Shang Li, Andrew C. Bryant, Howard Jiho Kim, Matthias Helmreich, Linda Stannieder, Zheng Tao, Qin Lichao, Sun Jieming, Yin Zhao, Du Zhijian, Yuan Zhongwei, Yuan Ta, Xie Xinyu, Liu Weiwei, Xiang Ling, Felipe Escudero, Sophia Tang, Diego Perez, Art Terry, Jtravis B Russett, Dustin Harris | Associate Engineers: China Institute of Building Standard Design & Research | Mechanical Engineer: The Institute of Shanxi Architectural Design and Research | Façade/cladding Consultants: SuP Ingenieure GmbH, Melendez & Dickinson Architects | Construction Contractor: Huhehaote construction Co., Ltd | Façade Contractor: Zhuhai King Glass Engineering Co. Ltd
Photography by Iwan Baan
pages 28–29

Manthey Kula
Norway | www.mantheykula.no
Roadside Restroom Akkarvikodden
Photography by Paul Warchol
pages 248–249

Manuelle Gautrand Architecture
France | www.manuelle-gautrand.com
La Cite Des Affaires
Credits: Manuelle Gautrand, representative architect; Thomas Daragon, works project manager; Yves Tougard, studies project manager | Firms involved: Structure: Khephren | Façade: Arcora | Maîtrise d'œuvre d'exécution: Debray Ingénierie | Main firms: Roofing/Finishings: Pitance-Lamy | Metallic framework: Baudin-Châteauneuf | Façade: Allouis
Photography: © Vincent Fillon (page 108, page 109/upper left image and bottom image), © Philippe Ruault (page 109/ middle left image and upper right image)
pages 108–109
—
C_42: Citroën Flagship Showroom
Photography: © Jimmy Cohrssen (upper left image), © Philippe Ruault (bottom left image, right image)
page 112
—
Origami Building
Credits: Manuelle Gautrand, principal architect; Yves Tougard, architect project manager | Interior design for Barclays: DGM Associés | Consultancy for green building standards: Cap Terre | HQE (High Environmental Quality) certification: Certivea | Construction Firms: Main structure: Colas | Curtain wall façades and exterior joinery: Schüco |

Double-skin, screenprinted glass and marble façades: Simetal
Photography: © Vincent Fillon
page 113
—
LaM—Lille Museum of Modern, Contemporary, and Outsider Art
Credits: Manuelle Gautrand, Representative Architect, Yves Tougard, Project manager Architect, joint Architect in Works phase | Museography: Renaud Pierard | Structures: Khephren | Fluids: Alto | Economist: LTA (studies phase), Guesquière-Dierickx (works phase) | Multimedia: Roger Labeyrie | Fire security: Casso
Photography: © Max Lerouge – LMCU
pages 140–141

Massimiliano & Doriana Fuksas
Italy | www.fuksas.it
Myzeil Shopping Mall
Interior Design: Fuksas Design | Engineering: Structures: Knippers-Helbig Beratende Ingenieure, Stuttgart; Krebs und Kiefer Beratende Ingenieure für das Bauwesen GmbH, Darmstadt | Realization of the façade and covering: Waagner Biro Stahlbau AG, Wien
Photography by Karsten Monnerjahn
pages 12–13
—
Admirant Entrance Building
Contractor: Heijmans Bouw | Realization of the covering: Waagner Biro Stahlbau AG, Wien | Structures: Knippers-Helbig Beratende Ingenieure, Stuttgart
Photography by Rob 't Hart (page 16/ upper image), Maggi Moreno (page 16/ bottom image, page 17)
pages 16–17

Mathieu Lehanneur
France | www.mathieulehanneur.fr
St. Hilaire Church
Mechanical engineering: Philippe Smith | Marble mason: Brocatelle
Photography by Felipe Ribon
pages 176–179
—
JWT Headquarters
Creative Team: Ana Moussinet, Pierre Favresse, Romain Guillet, Anne Doizy, Frederic Winckler
Photography by Véronique Huygue
pages 194–195
—
Studio 13/16, Centre Pompidou
Creative Team: Romain Guillet, Myriam Mortier, Cécile Fricker | In collaboration with LRa, Architects
Photography by Felipe Ribon
pages 204–205

Matsys
Andrew Kudless
USA | www.matsysdesign.com
P_Wall
Design and Fabrication Team: Chad Carpenter, Dino Rossi, Dan Robb, Frances Lee, Dorothy Leigh Bell, Janiva Ellis, Ripon DeLeon, Ryan Chandler, Ben Golder, Colleen Paz
Photography by Andrew Kudless
pages 150–151

Metaform Architecture
Luxembourg | www.metaform.lu
Apartment Building
Static Engineer: INCA, www.inca-ing.lu |
Artist: SUMO, www.sumo.lu
Photography by steve troes fotodesign
page 76

Mihály Balázs Architects
Mihály Balázs, Tamás Tarnóczky &
Balázs Tatár
Hungary
Regional Library and Knowledge Center
Photography by Tamás Bujnovszky
pages 218–219

MLRP
Denmark | www.mlrp.dk
Mirror House
Project leader: Robert Warren Paulsen |
Collaborators: Engineers: Grontmij A/S |
Landscape: GHB Landscape A/S |
Contractor: A.F.Hansen
Photography by Stamers Kontor,
www.stamerskontor.dk
pages 124–125

Neri & Hu Design and Research Office
China | www.neriandhu.com
The Waterhouse at South Bund
Design Team: Lyndon Neri, Rossana Hu,
Debby Haepers, Cai Chun yan, Markus
Stoecklein, Jane Wang | Contractors/
Consultants: Structure Consultants:
China Jingye Engineering Technology
Company | Mechanical Consultant:
Far East Consulting engineers
Limited | Kitchen Consultant: Polytek
Engineering Company Ltd.
Photography by Derryck Menere (page
138/left image and upper right image),
Tuomas Uusheimo (page 138/bottom
right image, page 139)
pages 138–139

NUCA Studio
Romania | www.nuca-studio.ro
Phill
Photography by Cosmin Dragomir
page 191

ODBC
Odile Decq
France | www.odbc-paris.com
**Phantom—Restaurant of the Garnier
Opera**
Author: Odile Decq – Odile Decq Benoit
Cornette Architectes Urbanistes |
Structure engineering: Batiserf
Ingénierie | Facade consultants: Odile
Decq – odile Decq Benoit Cornette
Architectes Urbanistes/HDA – Hugh
Dutton Associates | Building services
engineering: MS Consulting | Acoustics
engineering: Studio DAP | Fire security
engineering: SETEC | Kitchen consultants:
C2A Architectes | Project responsables:
Peter Baalman, Giuseppe Savarese,
Amélie Marchiset | Site: Garnier Opera,
Paris, France
Photography by Roland Halbe (page 196,
page 197/left images), ODBC (page 197/
right images)
pages 196–197

Office of Ryue Nishizawa
Japan | www.ryuenishizawa.com
Garden & House
Architect: Office of Ryue Nishizawa;
Design team: Ryue Nishizawa, Taeko
Nakatsub | Structural engineering:
structured environment – Alan Burden,
Hiroki Osanai | Construction supervision:
Heisei Construction – Hachiro Horigome,
Kim Daehwan Plant Enginee
Photography by Iwan Baan
pages 82–83
—
Teshima Art Museum
Photography by Iwan Baan
page 231

Olga Sanina & Marcelo Dantas
Portugal | osmd-a.com
The House of Books
Structural Engineer: Carlos Figueiredo
Photography by Miguel de Guzman
pages 210–211

Paul Le Quernec & Michel Grasso
*France | www.paul-le-quernec.fr | www.
michelgrasso.fr*
La Bulle Enchantée
Photography by Paul Le Quernec (page
24-25, page 27/left images and bottom
right image), Michel Grasso (page 26,
page 27/upper right image)
pages 24–27

Peter Zumthor & Louise Bourgeois
Steilneset: Witch Trial Memorial
Photography: ©Foto: Jarle Wæhler (page
240, page 241/upper left image and
bottom right image, page 242-243),
© Bjarne Riesto/www.riesto.no (page 241/
bottom left image and upper right image)
pages 240–243

**Phu Hoang Office & Rachely Rotem
Studio**
*USA | www.phuhoang.com |
www.rachelyrotem.com*
Exhale Pavilion
Project team: Phu Hoang, Rachely
Rotem, Ammr Vandal, Federica Von Euw,
Sunghyun Park
Photography by Robin Hill
page 159

Preston Scott Cohen, Inc.
USA | www.pscohen.com
**Herta and Paul Amir Building, Tel Aviv
Museum of Art**
Project Team: Preston Scott Cohen,
principal in charge of design, Amit
Nemlich, project architect; Tobias
Nolte, Bohsung Kong, project
assistants | Consultants: Structural
Engineers: YSS Consulting Engineers
Ltd., Dani Shacham | HVAC: M. Doron –
I. Shahar & Co., Consulting Eng.
Ltd. | Electrical: U. Brener – A. Fattal
Electrical & Systems Engineering Ltd. |
Lighting: Suzan Tillotson, New York
Photography by Amit Geron courtesy
Tel Aviv Museum of Art
pages 64–67

querkraft architekten
Jakob Dunkl, Gerd Erhartt & Peter Sapp
Austria | www.querkraft.at
TMW Technical Museum Vienna
Design and planning: dunkl, erhartt,
sapp. | Project architect: Dominique
Dinies | Project management: Dominique
Dinies | Project Team: Carmen Hottinger,
Lola Rieger, Robert Haranza, Lisi Wieser,
Christoph Fraundorfer, Aleca Bunescu,
Corinna Bach | Executive architect:
Querkraft ZT GmbH, Wien
Photography by Hertha Hurnaus/
Querkraft
pages 200–201

Ramón Esteve
Spain | www.ramonesteve.com
Myrtus Convention Center
Credits: Olga Badía, María Daroz, Daniela
Adame, Silvia M. Martínez, Emilio Pérez,
Gonzalo Llin, Juan Antonio Ferri
Photography by Eugeni Pons (page 198/
upper image, page 199/upper image and
bottom left image), Ramon Esteve Estudio
de Arquitectura (page 198/bottom image,
page 199/bottom right image)
pages 198–199

Reiulf Ramstad Architects
Norway | www.reiulframstadarkitekter.no
Trollwall Restaurant
Photography by Reiulf Ramstad
Architects
pages 122–123
—
**Trollstigen National Tourist Route
Project**
Credits: RRA Key Architects: Reiulf D
Ramstad – responsable project manager,
Christian Skram Fuglset – project
manager | RRA People involved in
process: Kristin Stokke Ramstad, project
communication; Anja Hole Strandskogen,
RRA architect; Espen Surnevik, RRA
architect; Ragnhild Snustad, RRA
architect; Atle Leira, RRA architect;
Kanog Anong Nimakorn, RRA architect;
Christian Dahle (former architect RRA);
Lasse A. Halvorsen, (former architect
RRA) | Civil Engineer: Structural
Engineer: Dr Techn. Kristoffer Apeland
AS, Oslo Norway
Photography by Reiulf Ramstad
Architects
page 247

Rintala Eggertsson Architects
Norway | www.rintalaeggertsson.com
Box Home
Sami Rintala, architect Oslo; Dagur
Eggertson, architect Oslo; John Roger
Holte, artist Oslo; Julian Fors, architect
student Vienna.
Sponsors: Aspelin-Ramm/funding;
Infill/funding; Ruukki/metal facades;
Pilkington Floatglass/windows;
Optimera Industri/interior wood; Vitra
Scandinavia/chair and lamps; SM-Lys/
lamps; Byggmakker/construction
material; Glava Isolasjon/insulation
Photography by Sami Rintala
page 77

RO&AD Architecten
Netherlands | www.ro-ad.org
Moses Bridge
Credits: Contributing architects:
Ro Koster, Ad Kil, Martin van
Overveld | Structural Engineer:
Adviesbureau Lüning
Photography by RO&AD Architecten
page 245

rojkind arquitectos & Esrawe Studio
*Mexico | www.rojkindarquitectos.com |
www.esrawe.com*
Tori Tori Restaurant
Credits: rojkind arquitectos: Michel Rojkind
(Founding Partner), Gerardo Salinas
(Partner); Project Team: Tere Levy, Agustín
Pereyra, Raúl Araiza, Carlos Alberto Ríos,
Isaac Smeke J., Enrique F. de la Barrera,
Daniela Bustamante, Daniel Hernández |
ESRAWE Studio: Héctor Esrawe (Principal
in Charge); Project Team: Ricardo Casas,
Basia Pineda, Ian Castillo, Karianne
Rygh, Alejandra Castelao, Jorge Bracho,
Rodrigo L. Franco | Design Computational
Consultants: Kokkugia (Roland Snooks,
Robert Stuart-Smith) | Construction: ZDA
desarrollo + arquitectura (Yuri Zagorin) |
Structural Engineering: Ing. Juan Felipe
Heredia | Facade Engineering: GRUPO
MAS (Ing. Eduardo Flores) | M.E.P.:
Quantum Diseño | Lightning Design: luz en
arquitectura (Arq. Kai Diederichsen) | Audio
& Video Design: NTX New Technology
Experience | Landscape Design: entorno
taller de paisaje | Furniture: Esrawe Studio |
Kitchen: San-Son | Visualization: ©
Glessner Group (www.glessnergroup.com) |
Interior Visualization: Esrawe Studio
Photography by Paúl Rivera – archphoto
pages 152–153

Ronan & Erwan Bouroullec
France | www.bouroullec.com
Textile Field
Photography by Studio Bouroullec & V&A
Images, Victoria and Albert Museum
page 203

Rudy Ricciotti
France | www.rudyricciotti.com
Jean Cocteau Museum
Architectural team: Architect:
Rudy Ricciotti, assisted by Marco
Arioldi | Lighting design: Lightec |
General construction engineering
design: SUDECO/Site driver:
Assouline | Acoustical engineering:
Thermibel | Landscape architect: APS
Paysagistes Associés | Front engineering:
Van Santen
Photography by Olivier Amsellem
page 37

Ryuji Nakamura
Japan | www.ryujinakamura.com
Bang
Credits: Direction: CNAC LAB
(CoSTUME NATIONAL Aoyama
Complex, www.cnac.jp)
Photography by Ryuji Nakamura &
Associates
page 146

Toyo Ito & Associates, Architects
Japan | www.toyo-ito.co.jp
Toyo Ito Museum of Architecture, Imabari
Credits: "Steel Hut" – Exhibition Building: Structural Engineers: SSC/Sasaki Structural Consultants | Mechanical Engineers: ES Associates Co., Ltd., Ohtaki E&M Consulting Office Co., Ltd. | General contractors: Taisei Corporation – "Silver Hut" – Archive/Workshop Building (Rebuilding Toyo Ito's own house): Structural Engineers: O.R.S. office | Mechanical Engineers: ES Associates, Ohtaki E&M Consulting Office Co., Ltd. | General contractors: Taisei Corporation
Photography by Sergio Pirrone
pages 98–99

UNStudio
Netherlands | www.unstudio.com
MUMUTH House for Music and Music Theater
Architect: UNStudio: Ben van Berkel, Caroline Bos with Hannes Pfau and Miklos Deri, Kirsten Hollmann, Markus Berger, Florian Pischetsrieder, Uli Horner, Albert Gnodde, Peter Trummer, Maarten van Tuijl, Matthew Johnston, Mike Green, Monica Pacheco, Ger Gijzen, Wouter de Jonge | Engineering: Arup London: Cecil Balmond, Volker Schmid, Charles Walker, Francis Archer.
Photography by Iwan Baan
pages 30–31
—

Burnham Pavilion
UNStudio: Ben van Berkel, Caroline Bos with Christian Veddeler, Wouter de Jonge and Hans-Peter Nuenning, Iona Sulea | Architects of Record: Garofalo Architects (Doug Garofalo with Grant Gibson) | On-Site Assembly/Deconstruction: Third Coast Construction (Dan Sheehy/Bryan Thomas) | Structural Engineer: Rockey Structures (Chris Rockey) | Official Steel Sponsor: ArcelorMittal
Photography by Christian Richters
pages 32–33
—

Galleria Centercity
Architect: UNStudio, Amsterdam; Design team: Ben van Berkel, Astrid Piber with Ger Gijzen, Marc Herschel and Marianthi Tatari, Sander Versluis, Albert Gnodde, Jorg Lonkwitz, Tom Minderhoud, Lee Jae-young, Woo Jun-seung, Constantin Boincean, Yu-chen Lin; Interior: Ben van Berkel, Astrid Piber with Ger Gijzen, Cristina Bolis and Veronica Baraldi, Lee Jae-young, Felix Lohrmann, Kirsten Hollmann, Albert Gnodde, Martijn Prins, Joerg Lonkwitz, Malaica Cimenti, Florian Licht, William de Boer, Grete Veskiväli, Eelco Grootjes, Alexia Koch | Executive Architect/Site Supervision/Landscape Architect: GANSAM Architects & Partners, Seoul, Korea; Design team: Kim Tai-jip, Han Ki-young, Nam Myung-kwan, Yoon Chang-bae, Park Seong-beom, Kwon Na-young, Nam Young-ho; Interior: Lee Seung-youn, No Se-hyo, Ryu Hee-won, Na Min-hee
Photography by Kim Yong-kwan
pages 156–157
—

Education Executive Agency & Tax Offices
UNStudio: Ben van Berkel, Caroline Bos and Gerard Loozekoot, with Jacques van Wijk, Frans van Vuure, Lars Nixdorff and Jesca de Vries, Ramon van der Heijden, Alicja Mielcarek, Eric den Eerzamen, Wendy van der Knijff, Machiel Wafelbakker, Timothy Mitanidis, Maud van Hees, Pablo Herrera Paskevicius, Martijn Prins, Natalie Balini, Peter Moerland, Arjan van der Bliek, Alexander Hugo, Gary Freedman, Jack Chen, Remco de Hoog, Willi van Mulken, Yuri Werner, René Rijkers, Machteld Kors, Leon Bloemendaal, Erwin Horstmanshof | Designteam: UNStudio, architecture and interior; Studio Linse, interior; Arup, structure, installations; Lodewijk Baljon, landscaping; Buro van Baar, wayfinding; YNNO, internal logistics
Photography by Ronald Tilleman (page 166/upper image, page 167/left image and upper right image), Aerophoto Eelde (page 166/bottom image), Christian Richters (page 167/bottom right image)
pages 166–167

Vazio S/A
Carlos Teixeira
Brazil | www.vazio.com.br
The Same, the Other
Photography by Nelson Kon
page 208

WAM Architecten
Wilfried van Winden
Netherlands | wam-architecten.nl
Hotel Inntel Zaandam
Credits: © design: WAM architecten/Molenaar & Van Winden architecten
Photography by Roel Backaert
pages 102–103

Wingårdh Arkitektkontor
Gert Wingårdh & Jonas Edblad
Sweden | www.wingardhs.se
Kuggen
Photography by Wingårdh Arkitektkontor AB
page 107

x architekten
Austria | www.xarchitekten.com
Hairstyle Interface
Photography by David Schreyer, www.architekturbild.net
page 147
—

Pastoral Care Center
Kunst am Bau: Gerhard Brandl
Photography by David Schreyer, www.architekturbild.net
pages 180–181

Yasutaka Yoshimura Architects
Japan | www.ysmr.com
Nowhere but Sajima
Client: Nowhere resort, www.nowhereresort.com
Photography by Yasutaka Yoshimura
pages 86–87

Zaha Hadid Architects
United Kingdom | www.zaha-hadid.com
London Aquatics Center
Design: Zaha Hadid Architects | Project Director: Jim Heverin | Project Architect: Glenn Moorley, Sara Klomps | Project Team: Alex Bilton, Alex Marcoulides, Barbara Bochnak, Carlos Garijo, Clay Shorthall, Ertu Erbay, George King, Giorgia Cannici, Hannes Schafelner, Hee Seung Lee, Kasia Townend, Nannette Jackowski, Nicolas Gdalewitch, Seth Handley, Thomas Soo, Tom Locke, Torsten Broeder, Tristan Job, Yamac Korfali, Yeena Yoon
Photography by Hufton + Crow
pages 20–21

The Sky's the Limit

Applying Radical Architecture

Edited by Robert Klanten, Sven Ehmann, and Sofia Borges
Text and preface by Sofia Borges

Cover and layout by Birga Meyer for Gestalten
Cover photography by David Franck
Typefaces: Hellschreiber Serif by Joerg Schmitt and
Malaussène Translation by Laure Afchain
Foundry: www.gestaltenfonts.com

Project management by Rebekka Wangler for Gestalten
Production management by Vinzenz Geppert for Gestalten
Proofreading by Rachel Sampson
Printed by Eberl Print, Immenstadt im Allgäu
Made in Germany

Published by Gestalten, Berlin 2012
ISBN 978-3-89955-422-9

For more information, please visit www.gestalten.com.

Bibliographic information published by the Deutsche Nationalbibliothek.
The Deutsche Nationalbibliothek lists this publication in the Deutsche
Nationalbibliografie; detailed bibliographic data are available online at
http://dnb.d-nb.de.

None of the content in this book was published in exchange for payment
by commercial parties or designers; Gestalten selected all included work
based solely on its artistic merit.

This book was printed on paper certified by the FSC®.

Gestalten is a climate-neutral company. We collaborate with the
non-profit carbon offset provider myclimate (www.myclimate.org)
to neutralize the company's carbon footprint produced through our
worldwide business activities by investing in projects that reduce CO_2
emissions (www.gestalten.com/myclimate).